Cognitive Development
A Functional Approach

Cognitive Development
A Functional Approach

Peter J. Valletutti, Ed. D.
Professor of Special Education
Virginia State University

Leonie Dummett, Ed. D.
Professor of Elementary Education
Virginia State University
Petersburg, Virginia

SINGULAR PUBLISHING GROUP, INC.
San Diego, California

Singular Publishing Group, Inc.
4284 41st Street
San Diego, California 92105-1197

© 1992 by Singular Publishing Group, Inc.

Printed in the United States of America by McNaughton & Gunn
Typeset in 10/12 Palatino by So Cal Graphics.

Library of Congress Cataloging-in-Publication Data

Valletutti, Peter J.
  Cognitive development: a functional approach/ by Peter J. Valletutti and
  Leonie Dummett.
        p.   cm.
  Includes bibliographical references and index.
  ISBN 1-879105-63-2
  1. Thought and thinking—Study and teaching—United States.
  2. Cognition in children–United States.   3. Handicapped children—Education—
  United States.
  I. Dummett, Leonie.   II. Title.
  LB1590.3.V35   1992
  370.15'2—dc20   92-10903
                                                                        CIP

CONTENTS

To my sisters-in-law, Mildred and Gloria Valletutti, for their love and support.

PJV

To my wonderful brother, friend, and benefactor, Lloyd G. Smith, whose love, kindness, and devotion have enabled me to succeed.

LD

PREFACE

Cognitive Development: A Functional Approach has been written for preservice and inservice teachers and trainers as well as any person who needs to learn how cognitive skills can be taught and developed through relevant, well-planned, functional activities in the school, home, and community. The aim of this book is to help all teachers, especially those who teach students with disabilities, to become more effective in assisting students in developing their cognitive abilities to the fullest. This text is particularly appropriate for use in teaching methodology courses that address the special educational needs of learners with moderate and severe disabilities. It is also relevant for those courses that explore curriculum development and instructional planning and implementation strategies for very young to adult learners with mild disabilities. Teachers working in mainstreamed and other regular classrooms should also find this book beneficial. Nondisabled as well as disabled learners are likely to make significant progress when a functional approach to learning is pursued. This is because it is a highly motivating and stimulating approach to cognitive development and the acquisition of essential, reality-based knowledge, concepts, values, and skills.

All educators are familiar with the cognitive domain and understand its importance to all aspects of learning. Three problems exist, however. The first is that cognitive skills are usually taught as ends in themselves rather than as means to enable students to function in all areas of their lives in and out of school. The second problem is that many instructors teach special education students as though they cannot think and, therefore, do not need to develop higher levels of cognition. The third problem is that teachers frequently forget that all the activities of daily living, even the most basic and most simple, in and out of the classroom, call for the use of cognitive operations. Most special education students can develop and use their cognitive abilities if teachers and trainers employ the functional approach.

Functional curricula and functional methods of instruction necessary for the implementation of functional curricula require that knowledge, skills, and concepts be learned in and through practical applications in real-life situations. Through the use of real-life settings and materials, it is expected that students will acquire meaning from their life experiences. As a result of learning through a functional approach, students will be able to apply their knowledge, skills, values, and concepts to their present and future experiences.

Any educational text for the 21st century must address and attempt to offer solutions for the serious problems facing education as well as society in general. Today, countless students are leaving school functionally illiterate. These and other "at-risk" students put the entire nation at-risk. Many National Assessment of Educational Progress reports, as well as other studies, have noted the same problem: namely, students lack the ability to translate the bits and pieces of facts they learn in school into solving problems and analyzing and evaluating information in order to make judgments or decisions crucial to their lives. In short, they are unable to think critically. This book focuses on students as active members of society who must constantly use their cognitive abilities to process all types of oral and written information in order to meet the demands of life. This book also stresses the importance and effectiveness of using the functional approach to help students develop the cognitive domain. It also stresses the importance of critical thinking in the total education of students.

This text presents a balance between theory and applications for developing cognition through the functional approach. Chapters 1 through 3 present Cognitive Development, the Functional Approach, and Informal Educational Assessment and Instructional Planning. Each chapter from 4 through 6 covers a cognitive category and the functional approach to teaching that category. Each chapter also contains lessons illustrating how that particular category can be taught from a functional perspective. In Chapters 7 through 12, the functional approach is applied to six topics involving cognitive processes. In each of these chapters, particular cognitive processes are illustrated and a lesson is provided to demonstrate how each can be taught through the use of functional activities.

PART I

COGNITIVE DEVELOPMENT, A FUNCTIONAL APPROACH, AND ASSESSMENT

The first section of this book focuses on cognitive development, the functional approach, and informal educational assessment and instructional planning. Cognitive development is extremely important to learning. Instructors at all levels need to understand how to stimulate, encourage, and sustain cognitive development. Chapter 1 covers the stages of cognitive development and delineates various underlying attributes of each stage. Special emphasis is placed on schema theory and metacognition.

Cognitive development does not take place in a vacuum. It occurs in the context of various types of environments. The more relevant and pragmatic the environment, the more efficiently and naturally students' level of cognition will evolve. Chapter 2 describes how this can be accomplished through a functional approach. The chapter defines the functional approach and explains its importance in the instruction of all students, particularly those with special needs. This chapter attempts to underscore that cognitive input is required to perform all the activities in which people engage in daily living; therefore, these activities may be used effectively to enhance cognitive development.

This first section also deals with evaluation and instructional planning. The emphasis is that alternative means of assessing students are necessary, replacing formal instruments that are so frequently overused and applied inappropriately. Several alternate informal educational assessment strategies are proffered in this section.

1

COGNITIVE
DEVELOPMENT

This chapter is by no means a comprehensive discussion of cognitive development. It is rather, a brief discussion of the subject with particular reference to how cognition develops and the developmental implications for teaching and learning.

One of the greatest natural endowments of humans is the ability to acquire knowledge. However, the acquisition of knowledge does not occur instantaneously and at a single moment of time at the beginning of life. Rather, this process of "knowing" occurs in developmental stages. Each cognitive stage precipitates the next one and overlaps with it. Cognitive development is as vital to the well-being of the individual as is physical and emotional development. As children interact with and adapt to the environment while they attempt to make sense out of the wide range of experiences they encounter, they begin to construct their own view of the world. No one else can "learn" the world for them. Each individual is unique and must come to terms with the environment in his or her own unique way. The way children develop cognitively, however, is directly related to the type of environment provided for them. The environment may stimulate and encourage cognitive growth or stifle and delay it. According to Smith, Goodman, and Meredith (1976), cognitive development definitely affects emotional development. They suggest that, if children's cognitive relationship to the world is impaired, they may carry the early acquired misconceptions into adult life. These misconceptions can have adverse effects on the way individuals adjust to the world emotionally.

There is also a very vital relationship between cognitive development and learning. Burns, Roe, and Ross (1984) suggest that the child's cognitive developmental level is more important for learning than is his or her mental age. Those who assume the responsibility for helping children acquire knowledge and learn how to learn, must understand how cognitive growth takes place, the kinds of environment that provide optimum stimulation, and the role of teachers and trainers in the development of cognitive competence. Educators, parents, and other caregivers should make sure that the child's cognitive development is not left to chance during any stage of his or her life. Research indicates that important relationships exist between cognitive processing and achievement. It also suggests that cognitive confusion is a major reason for early failure in school (Downing, 1972).

Many incorrect assumptions have been held about how and what children learn during the teaching process. Misconceptions on how children's mental faculties develop and how they learn can result in misdiagnosis, inaccurate labeling, and the use of inappropriate methods and materials of instruction. This produces a vicious cycle that creates more cognitive damage. If teachers and trainers understand the process of cognitive growth and how children learn, they will be able to provide the types of strategies and programs that will stimulate and foster the cognitive process and prevent cognitive confusion and impairment that may cause serious problems (Holdaway, 1979).

Children's cognitive development affects how they learn, understand, store knowledge, characterize and interpret information, see relationships between and among ideas, retain and retrieve information, use prior knowledge to gain new knowledge, and utilize knowledge in functional contexts. It is very important, therefore, as Piaget (1964) stated, for teachers to understand that: "The goal in education is not to increase the amount of knowledge but to create the possibilities for a child to invent and discover" (p. 3). This suggestion redefines the role of teachers and trainers. In helping children grow and develop their mental abilities to the fullest, teachers and trainers should not function as information dispensers, but as facilitators who create the type of climate that will stimulate children to question, discover, and learn without unnecessary input or unwarranted control from adults.

COGNITION

A discussion of cognitive development would be meaningless without an analysis of what is involved in cognition. In its broadest sense, cognition involves all the mental processes that result in knowing and in building knowledge. It includes perception, thinking, remembering, learning, and problem solving. Eisenson and Ogilvie (1983) indicate that cognition also involves language, as it is through language that children "codify" the results of their cognitive processes. They further suggest that cognitive processing in children includes not only learning how to learn but also how to become proficient in obtaining and using knowledge.

Many theorists have contributed to our understanding of cognition (Bruner, 1962; Flavell, 1963; Guildford, 1967; Hunt, 1961; Sigal & Hooper, 1968; Vygotsky, 1934, 1962). In Guildford's view, cognition involves the instantaneous discovery and perception of information in different forms. The individual who has contributed most to our understanding of cognition, however, is Jean Piaget. Much of the research done by these authors has been motivated by his work. His ideas have greatly influenced the thinking of educators concerning the way children learn and think. For Piaget (1964), cognition is the internal adjustment that the child makes to the external world. This involves the comprehensive process of discovery, awareness, assimilation, and the adaptation that children go through as they adjust to the environment. Piaget believed that as the child interacts with his or her environment, the youngster develops neural systems or structures of conceptualizing which enable him or her to understand and acquire knowledge. Each individual's structure is unique and is altered as new learning takes place.

Piaget's theories have been studied by many researchers. Among them are Flavell (1963) and Hunt (1961). In Flavell's summaries of Piaget's theories, he suggests that Piaget views cognition as a creative process of building new structures on prior ones. This constructive process is the development of cognition.

HOW COGNITION DEVELOPS

In Piaget's view, cognitive development occurs in stages and involves both thought and language. He saw thought as coming before language, with language acting as the external agent that the child uses as he or she explores and adapts to the environment (1964). He outlined four stages of cognitive growth: *sensorimotor, preoperational, concrete operational,* and *formal operational*. Prior to discussing each stage, it is necessary to describe the mental processes involved in learning how to think. This must be done to ascertain what is occurring during each stage and also to understand what precipitates the climax of one stage and the preparation for the beginning of another stage.

Five important terms are frequently used in conjunction with the development and change associated with each stage. They are: *structure, schemata, assimilation, accommodation,* and *metacognition*.

The manner in which knowledge is organized in the brain is referred to as cognitive structure. Knowledge, however, is not randomly organized. It is arranged in categories analogous to a file system. These categories are called SCHEMATA or STRUCTURES (Tompkins & Hoskisson, 1991). A single category is called a schema. The schemata consist of three components: categories of knowledge, a system of rules for determining what makes up a category and what should be incorporated in it, and the web of interrelationships within the categories. These schemata, or clusters of thought, are not mere linear segmented expansions of stimulus–response combinations. Rather, they function as totally integrated systems in which the whole exceeds the sum of the parts (Smith et al., 1976). As children grow cognitively, they add schemata and as they learn they develop new categories.

Although people may have similar categories, each individual's schemata are unique because they are based on personal experiences and interests (Tompkins & Hoskisson, 1991). For example, some people may put their knowledge of alligators, chickens, cows, cats, dogs, lions, tigers, horses, and snakes into one category—animals. Other individuals using their knowledge and experience may separate the list into categories and subcategories—mammals and nonmammals, herbivorous and carnivorous, and so on. Those who would categorize animals in the latter manner would be able to do so because they had learned a set of rules related to the distinctive characteristics of each animal. Individuals, knowing these characteristics, can classify the animals and place them into a particular group. Stauffer(1969) asserts: "We do not inherit cognitive structures but a way of transacting cognitive business with our environment" (p. 310).

As children interact with and adjust to their environment they acquire new information. This necessitates expanding existing categories or creating new ones. Two important terms are used to describe the processes of constructing new schemata. They are assimilation and accommodation (Piaget, 1969).

When children encounter novel situations, new information is ASSIMILATED into previous related data; concurrently, these previous ideas are ACCOMMODATED to the new (Smith et al., 1976). Tompkins & Hoskisson (1991) define assimilation as, "The cognitive process by which information from the environment is integrated into existing schemata. In contrast, accommodation is the cognitive process by which existing schemata are modified or new schemata are restructured to adapt to the environment" (p. 4). Through these two processes children add new ideas to their concept of the world and alter their concept of the world as a result of encountering new information. Piaget (1964) believed that assimilation is crucial to the learning process. He affirmed, "I shall define assimilation as the integration of any sort of reality into a structure, and it is this assimilation which seems to me fundamental in learning" (p. 18).

Assimilation and accommodation operate as a unitary process. An idea that is assimilated is also accommodated. These two processes of mental adaptation make cognitive development possible. As new ideas are assimilated and accommodated into existing meaning structures, the structures change, making it possible for more new information to be accommodated. This continuous process is the vital force behind cognitive growth. The rate of growth, however, is dependent on prior experiences. The individual can assimilate only those new ideas and experiences which earlier experiences have prepared the individual to accommodate. If the new information is meaningful, it is more easily assimilated into existing schemata (Stauffer, 1969). Once cognitive structures are built, according to Flavell (1963), "they apply themselves again and again to the assimilable aspects of the environment" (p. 55).

According to Smith et al. (1976) children's schemata are extended and enriched as they add new data to previously learned information and as they analyze, conceptualize, and utilize prior knowledge in slightly different ways. Novel relationships between and among old ideas evolve as children discover and encounter different aspects of a prior concept. For example, a child in the concrete operational stage may classify dogs, cats, pigs, and cows as "animals—that is, nonhuman," in a farm situation. When the youngster visits a zoo and sees lions, tigers, and coyotes for the first time, however, he or she assimilates the concept of these particular animals into his or her category of "animals" and then adds to his or her prior knowledge of animals by noting some differences regarding these particular animals' habitats and temperament. They now understand that these creatures in the zoo are also animals, but that they are different from the animals on the farm. The zoo animals have to live in cages because they are wild or dangerous. Later in the formal operational period, more changes occur in the child's conceptualization of "animals;" rather than lumping all animals into a single category by using one attribute, "nonhuman," this individual is now able to separate animals into classes and subclasses based on rules regarding distinctive characteristics: for example, farm animals and wild animals, mammals and nonmammals, vertebrates and invertebrates, and herbivorous and carnivorous. Thus, a new kind of cognitive process has expanded and made the previous simpler schema more complex. The individual in the formal operational stage can retain the concept of animals as nonhuman while classifying them as mammals, and so on. This illustrates the process of schemata expansion, development, and enrichment.

What initiates this cognitive growth process? Piaget (1975) suggested that cognitive development is induced by the process of EQUI-

LIBRIUM. DISEQUILIBRIUM, or conflict, occurs when children encounter new information they cannot assimilate into existing schemata. This produces cognitive confusion which forces them to seek equilibrium, that is, adjust to the environment. If the child's schemata is able to adjust to the new information, the disequilibrium precipitated by the new experience will stimulate the child to learn. If, however, the child cannot accommodate the new information, learning will not occur (Tompkins & Hoskisson, 1991). This has important implications for teachers of all children, but especially for those who teach children with learning problems. Teachers and trainers should develop methods and materials that, on the one hand, will be sufficiently challenging to motivate students to activate their schemata and use their prior knowledge to gain new ideas but, on the other hand, are not so easy that they fail to provide the motivation needed to acquire new information.

Another important concept associated with cognitive development is METACOGNITION. Norton (1989) defines it as, "an individual's knowledge of the functions of his or her own mind and the conscious efforts to monitor or control those functions" (p. 35). Children must be taught how to monitor their own learning. Teachers and trainers should encourage children to ask themselves questions like, "Do I understand? Am I learning? Is this clear? Am I using the best strategies available? What steps should I take to clarify this concept and retain it? How much of this information do I understand?" When children are engaged in this process, it not only helps to keep them focused, it also motivates them to activate prior knowledge and use it to learn new information. The five processes discussed above are very important to an understanding of cognitive development and learning.

THE ENVIRONMENT AND COGNITIVE DEVELOPMENT

The process of cognitive development is not self-sustaining. It is maintained by meaningful activity within the child's environment. The process is cyclical. Cognitive schemata are constructed through action, that is, by functioning, and continue to perpetuate schematic processes by functioning. However, functioning does not occur in a vacuum. An environment is needed to provide both the stimulus and the raw materials for building cognitive structures.

An inherent feature of schemata building is that once the schemata are constructed, they continuously assimilate and accommodate anything in the environment that is assimilable (Stauffer, 1969). Both assimilation and accommodation need an environment in which to function. Flavell (1963) affirms, "the principal attribute of assimilation is *repetition*—the intrinsic tendency to reach out into the environment again and again and incorporate what it can" (p. 79). It is apparent, therefore, that the environment is directly related to the construction of schemata. The degree to which cognitive growth takes place is dependent on the quality of the environment. The environment nourishes, sustains, and provides the elements as well as the incentive for cognitive growth. The individual's cognitive development is shaped by the experiences that the environment provides.

If the environment is impoverished and is not conducive to cognitive growth, children's mental growth will be thwarted. This will produce negative effects throughout the individual's life. Smith et al. (1976) suggest, "Positive cognitive activity is as essential to well-being as are physical activity and the exercise of the emotions. If children do not accomplish cognitive adjustment to the world, they may maintain into maturity misconceptions that can adversely affect their emotional adjustment" (p. 87). This presents serious implications for education because the learning environment affects not only cognitive development but the way the child conceptualizes the world. The classroom environment may promote, delay, or impair cognitive growth. A "rich" nonthreatening, stimulating environment is, perhaps, one of the most important factors in facilitating cognitive development. An environment conducive to cognitive growth is one in which students encounter situations that incite their curiosity and inspire them to think, explore, discover, question, experiment, make mistakes, and monitor their own learning.

LANGUAGE AND COGNITIVE DEVELOPMENT

Piaget (1964) believed that language plays a crucial role in cognitive development. In his view, language is the external agent in the child's development of thought. It enables the child to translate thought into meaning as the youngster relates to the environment. Thought structures are first built by observation and manipulation before the individual is able to deal with the symbolic representation of language.

As children go from actions to images, and then to words, the development of language enhances their ability to organize ideas and experiences more meaningfully. As an integral part of the individual's process of experiencing and knowing, language becomes the embodiment of thought. Smith et al., (1976) state, "the thing is not known until it is named and its interrelationship with other things is not understood until language embodies the idea" (p. 84). In continuing their discussion on language and the ideation process, these authors further suggest, "Language frames the thought and imbues it with communicable meaning so that it may be held in memory and used again in interplay with other thoughts" (p. 111). Cognitive development involves the constant interaction between interrelated experiences and languages.

In the early stage of cognitive development, many environmental cues are nonverbal. However, language is central to the formation of concepts as well as images. Language, in Bruner's (1962) view, is not just a medium of communication, it is the mechanism of thought. The young child's thoughts are molded to a large extent by conversations with him- or herself and with others in the environment. As the individual builds cognitive structures into which he or she assimilates and accommodates new information, language shapes thought while thought creates the individual's private perception of his or her world through language. Research (Stauffer, 1969) indicates that as children grow cognitively they rely heavily on language to translate knowledge into functioning operations and also to engage in problem-solving activities. In Tompkins and Hoskissons' (1991) view language assists children in learning about their world and in understanding it. Language is, therefore, central to cognitive development.

STAGES IN COGNITIVE DEVELOPMENT

Piaget (1963) described four general stages through which children go as they develop cognitively—*sensorimotor, preoperational, concrete operational,* and *formal operational.*

The SENSORIMOTOR, or PREVERBAL STAGE, extends approximately from birth to 2 years of age. During this period, the child adjusts to his or her environment through motor actions. Understanding at this stage is nonverbal and quite simple.

Children at this stage are rather egocentric. They make little effort to think about their own thoughts or to adapt their speech to their listeners (Stauffer, 1969). They are also unable to deal with different attributes of an element at the same time. Attention is focused on a single feature, and their actions are limited to reality. These children cannot deal with successive changes in an operation because the assimilatory and accommodative mechanisms are not sufficiently developed to cope with this task.

The PREOPERATIONAL STAGE extends approximately from age 2 to 7. A child in this stage differs from a child in the previous stage, primarily because the youngster is able to function on a representational level rather than on a simple "direct action" level. During this period, children can manipulate and organize different aspects of their world more effectively. They acquire the ability to deal with written language, which now becomes an important tool in exploring the environment, acquiring new information, and communicating through reading and writing.

Children at this stage are rapidly developing concepts but are not able to think logically. They group and categorize things on a functional basis. For example, they may combine spoon with cereal and ice cream because one uses a spoon to eat both. These children also lack the concept of conservation of substance—the idea that something may remain inherently the same, despite changes in its size or form. They have difficulty, for example, in understanding that a short, wide glass contains the same amount of liquid as a tall, slim one or that a single coin, the nickel, is the same as five single pennies. The more models these children have to imitate and the more enriching their environment, the more likely they will develop intellectually during this period.

The CONCRETE OPERATIONAL STAGE extends approximately from age 7 to 11. During this period, children are capable of performing various operations, but they can do so only with concrete objects. At this stage, they are beginning to understand the concept of conservation and reversibility. They can observe an operation, change it, and then return it to its original form. During this period, they are capable of reasoning about things they have read if those things are directly related to their experiences (Burns et al., 1984). They are more proficient in their use of language and can read and understand things that are readily related to their environment.

The FORMAL OPERATIONAL STAGE appears between the ages of 11 and 15. During this stage, a very important transformation takes place. Children are now able to think in abstract terms about ideas that are unrelated to their direct experiences. They are also able to use their thoughts to direct and explain their observations. They can now produce ideas about ideas. They are no longer limited to those ideas that deal with the real and the concrete. They can now handle hypothetical and abstract experiences. Hunt (1961) says, a child operating in this stage, "can consider hypotheses which may or may not be true, and consider what would follow if they were true. He can follow the form of an argument while disregarding its concrete content" (pp. 230–231).

These four stages of cognitive development must not be conceptualized as separate "epochs" which are fixed and unrelated to one another. Each stage is characterized by specific cognitive functions in which there is continuous transformations as schemata are being constructed and reconstructed. The development of a previous stage affects the stage that follows. Piaget believed that the cognitive stages are related to biological development and that each stage emerges in a sequential order and is connected to a previous one. The order of each is not reversible, and no stage can be avoided. For example, a child cannot go through the formal operational stage before he or she has gone through the sensorimotor stage. Nor can the child completely avoid going through a particular stage. Some children may complete a stage or all the stages more quickly or more slowly than others, but all children pass through the stages in the same order. These stages of development must not be viewed merely as periods or ages when certain behaviors are exhibited by the child. They must be seen as representations of the style of thinking the child uses to explore his or her environment (Smith et al., 1976).

Many variables affect the rate at which children move through each stage. Some of these are: innate capacity, physical health, the quality of the environment and background experiences, and language facility. Educators and other caregivers must also be aware that although a group of children are at the same chronological and mental age, it does not necessarily mean that they are functioning at the same cognitive level. Parents, teachers, and trainers must bear in mind both the possibilities and limitations of each stage and provide the kinds of experiences that will stimulate and enhance cognitive development at a particular period.

COGNITIVE DEVELOPMENT AND
THE CHILD WITH LEARNING PROBLEMS

No analysis of cognitive development would be complete without a brief discussion concerning children with learning problems. Students with learning problems often exhibit deficiencies particularly at the higher levels necessary for imagery, verbal processing, and concept formation (Norton, 1989). Kavale (1980) found that children with learning disabilities frequently experience difficulties comprehending concepts related to quantity, time, and space. Torgesen (1979) discovered deficiencies with memory and the development of retention strategies.

Teachers and trainers need to provide activities that will help these children to arrange, classify, and structure information into meaningful wholes. Semantic mapping activities will also help them visualize relationships among concepts (Myers, 1983). Because of the complex nature of learning disabilities and because children with learning disabilities vary widely, classroom teachers and trainers must provide a wide variety of teaching strategies to meet the needs of all these children. No one method of teaching would effectively meet the needs of all children with learning disabilities. It is equally important to provide reinforcement activities and strategies that will build students' self-esteem and provide them with success. The strengths developed from successfully mastering prior cognitive tasks should be utilized to encourage the development of other skills. This is important for all children, but especially for children with learning problems and disabilities.

Cognitive development is as important for children with learning problems as it is for other children. That these students have special needs and employ different learning strategies does not mean that they process information and acquire knowledge in a noncognitive way. *Whenever a functional approach is used in teaching these children, educators must be cognizant that all functional tasks require some level of assimilation and application of knowledge.* Even those skills performed automatically required the construction of schemata when the individual encountered those tasks initially. *Teachers and trainers must not indulge themselves in the misconception (or allow others to) that cognitive development relates only to students without learning disabilities or that the performance of functional skills does not require cognitive skills.* Special students, on the contrary, by the very nature of their limitations need well-planned, structured, creative, repetitive, carefully spaced, and practical programs to assist them in the development of those cognitive skills necessary to the performance of everyday tasks that other students may perform easily. These children need many opportunities to overlearn by continuing to practice a skill even after mastery is achieved to ensure retention and understanding. Emphasis must be placed on functional skills that these individuals need in order to live as successfully as possible. They should be involved in learning activities that foster the highest level of cognitive development of which they are capable.

IMPLICATIONS FOR EDUCATION

The principal implications of Piaget's theory of cognitive development are:

1.   Children should be allowed to do their own learning. They learn more effectively by being active participants in the learning process than by passively listening to teachers and memorizing facts. Teachers must plan instruction and create learning environments based on the concept that children learn better when they are encouraged to manipulate objects, explore, experiment, construct, question, and discover and reconcile what they discover at one time with what they dis-

cover at another time. It is necessary to reiterate Piaget's (1964) statement which was quoted earlier in this chapter. He said, "The goal in education is not to increase the amount of knowledge but to create the possibilities for the child to invent and discover" (p. 3).

2. The manner in which children process thoughts differs at various stages in their development. Teachers and trainers should consider cognitive development levels as they plan curricula for children in a particular stage of development.

3. As children relate to their environment and attempt to understand it, they learn by relating previously learned information to new information. Educators should plan instruction that will assist students in relating the known to the unknown. They should not expect children to learn successfully if they have no prior experience on which to build the new information. The amount and complexity of new information presented in a particular lesson should be within the student's ability to assimilate and accommodate. If children are presented with information that is beyond their range of understanding, negative disequilibrium will occur. When cognitive conflicts arise that they cannot resolve in a relatively short period of time, they are likely to become discouraged and give up trying.

It is the responsibility of teachers and trainers to evaluate the content of instructional materials in terms of the individual's previous experiences, the cognitive operation(s) involved in performing the task, and the individual's level of intellectual functioning. Teachers must prepare programs so that the difficulty of the content to be learned is presented in the proper sequence to coincide with the child's level of cognitive growth. New information should be presented in meaningful contexts and should be sufficiently novel to encourage the student to try to process it, and yet, it should not be so difficult that it causes frustration. Too many frustrating experiences are likely to discourage further attempts to process new information (Tompkins & Hoskisson, 1991). Teachers and trainers should provide various opportunities for review and reinforcement. They should also give students *wait time.* Children need silence to think. Teachers need to allow time for students to think about ideas, formulate questions, and construct answers that are both convergent and divergent. This helps students to develop higher level thinking skills. Teachers and trainers should be alert to *teachable moments* when children indicate interest in or readiness for

learning new concepts or for extending old ones, even though these occasions were not initiated by the teacher.
4.   Cognitive development is facilitated by peer interaction. Children need not only interaction with adults but also with their peers. Piaget emphasized the importance of having children interact with other children functioning at the same level. This kind of interaction helps to liberate youngsters from their egocentrism and enables them to gain perspective. As children communicate with one another, they become aware that other people share their ideas or have ideas that differ from theirs. This gives them a perspective they would not gain otherwise. For educators, this means planning meaningful group activities that provide opportunities for discussing, planning, sharing, brainstorming, conducting experiments, and participating in other activities that will encourage children to work cooperatively in meaningful ways. In order for children to obtain maximum benefits from peer interaction, however, teachers must provide guidance, but they must operate more as facilitators than as controllers of the learning situation.

COGNITIVE DEVELOPMENT ACTIVITIES

Here it is necessary to reiterate the fact that children learn by *doing*. They must be actively involved in the learning situation. This is true for all children, but is especially true of youngsters with special needs. It is essential that teachers and trainers prepare activities and strategies that will facilitate cognitive development. Educators need to prepare appropriate innovative activities that will enable all children to experience success.

Some strategies and activities that enhance cognitive development include:

1.   Encourage students to use concrete objects—noting size, color, weight, texture, and function;
2.   Encourage students to take objects such as a simple toy apart and then reassemble it;
3.   Encourage students to separate objects into groups according to size, form, color, and function;
4.   Encourage students to match objects that belong together such as socks and shoes;
5.   Ask students to separate objects that are alike from those that are different—for example, ask them to put all dark clothes and white clothes into separate piles for laundering;

6. Encourage children to classify things according to their function—for example, ask them to put all eating utensils in the kitchen and all grooming supplies and equipment in the bathroom;

7. Give the students opportunities to work with the concept of conservation—for example, place two identical rows of quarters in front of them, spread out one row so that the quarters in this row are further apart than those in the other row. Ask the students whether the rows still have the same number of quarters;

8. Place equal amounts of fruit juice into two tall, thin glasses. Pour the juice from one glass into a short, wide glass. Ask the students if the two glasses still have the same amount.

To help students develop higher cognitive levels, teachers and trainers may continue to provide similar activities at more complex levels. They must also involve students in word–thought association activities that will enhance observational skills. Teachers may, for example, show pictures that illustrate different emotions. After students have had sufficient time for *observation,* ask them to describe not only the feelings observed in the pictures but occasions in which they have experienced these emotions.

Students may also be asked to make *comparisons.* For example, they may compare the attributes of clothing versus things that are not clothing. They may also compare the characters in two different stories, or they may compare the functions of people working in different service occupations.

Another important activity is *hypothesizing.* Children may observe the headline on a newspaper article and hypothesize about the contents. Older students may be expected to hypothesize about cause and effect situations in which the cause is presented and they must identify possible effects or what they think the likely effect might be.

Organizing activities are also very useful. Students need many opportunities to develop their concept about time sequence and identify the order in which things take place. Several well-known stories can be used repeatedly to help students understand this concept, for example: *The Three Little Pigs* in which the wolf went from the flimsiest house to the strongest house; *The Three Billy Goats Gruff* which illustrates sequence according to size from smallest to the largest; and *The Little Red Hen* which illustrates chronological order in the steps for preparing the bread.

The final activity concerns *application.* Students need lots of practice in applying the knowledge they have gained in different situations. They should be encouraged to observe, experiment, construct things, gather data, demonstrate, compare and contrast objects and ideas, follow directions to complete a process, formulate hypotheses, and find solutions to problems. Brainstorming and other discussions are very useful in stimulating cognitive development capabilities. The activities discussed above are excellent for cognitive development. They do not, however, in any way represent an exhaustive list. Teachers and trainers can develop hundreds of activities under the basic categories outlined above. Students need a wide variety of experiences in order to develop cognitive competence at each stage.

SUMMARY

Cognitive development is crucial to learning. It affects the way the child and later the adult views the world. Cognitive development proceeds in an orderly manner, with each stage displaying specific abilities. No stage can be omitted. How efficiently cognition develops is directly related to the quality of the environment. Children do not inherit cognitive structures or schemata but the facility to construct them, using the meaningful elements in the environment. Children learn best when they actively participate in the learning situation. They must be at the center of the learning process; only then will they learn what they can incorporate into their knowledge bank. Teachers should create learning environments that will stimulate children's cognitive development. Their role is central to the learning process, because they prepare the environment, develop strategies, and set the general stage for learning. While they cannot supply cognitive growth (the child must grow for him- or herself), they can endeavor to understand how it progresses and nurture it by creating the conditions and materials conducive to its development. If educators want to know what opportunities will best encourage cognitive development, they must understand the child's cognitive potential at each stage of development. There is no single ideal strategy that will suit all children.

Intellectual functioning requires a balance between the person and his or her environment. Interaction between children and their peers and also adults is of primary importance. This interaction enables children to acquire rationality, objectivity, and a holistic view of the world. Maximum development at each stage is assured if opportunities are provided for children to think and develop schemata. Understanding cognitive development is of primary importance to teachers and trainers because it is crucial to learning and to the way children perceive the world and how they will function later as adults.

2

THE FUNCTIONAL
APPROACH

DEFINING THE FUNCTIONAL APPROACH

The functional approach to educating students with disabilities and those who are nondisabled involves both a philosophy of education that shapes the contents of a life skills curriculum and an instructional strategy that determines the nature of its delivery (Bender & Valletutti, 1985; Valletutti & Bender, 1985). According to Kirk and Gallagher (1989), "Over the years, from research, common sense, and experience, a philosophy of teaching students with multiple and severe handicaps has evolved. Today our objective is to teach functional age-appropriate skills within the integrated school and non-school settings, and to base our teaching on the systematic evaluation of students' progress" (p. 467).

As an *educational philosophy*, the functional approach identifies essential life skills and then seeks to enable student adaptation to the requirements of daily existence through the acquisition of these skills. It is adult-referenced in that it is based on a top-down strategy that identifies those elements necessary for successful community adjustment rather than a bottom-up strategy which has an elementary-oriented focus (Polloway, Patton, Payne, & Payne, 1989). It pursues the development of those skills that foster autonomy when independence is appropriate, as in self-care activities, and codependence when cooperation is appropriate, as in problem solving in the home and in completing sequential and interrelated tasks in the workplace. It endeavors to develop situation-specific skills that will allow students

19

to be as successful and productive and have as enjoyable a life as possible as they function on a daily basis.

As an *instructional strategy*, the functional approach shapes the instructional process. A curriculum that is designed and developed from a functional perspective requires that specified functional skills be taught functionally. That is, they either are to be taught directly through actual experiences in the home, school, or community, or may be taught vicariously through classroom simulations that capture reality contexts. What is taught must include activities that are community-referenced—those that are needed in specific home, community, vocational, and leisure environments. Once teachers and trainers identify and thoroughly analyze the requirements of specific environments, they can then prepare students for living in those communities. Instructors must determine specific performance requirements and teach specifically to these requirements, and, whenever possible, teach them as practiced in actual locations (Brown, Nietupski, & Hamre-Nietupski, 1976; Polloway et al., 1989).

Conducting an ecological inventory has been suggested as a strategy for generating a functional curriculum that is community-referenced. The steps involved in this process include: identifying curriculum domains (vocational, domestic living, community living, and leisure); describing present and future environments and subenvironments; clarifying and prioritizing the activities pertinent to these environments; specifying the skills needed to perform these activities; conducting a discrepancy analysis to determine required skills currently not in the student's behavioral repertoire; determining needed adaptations in student performance; and, finally, developing the individualized instructional program (Brown, Branston et al., 1979; Brown, Branston-McLean et al., 1979).

A functional curriculum presents *what* is to be taught while the functional approach to instruction determines *how* a skill should be taught. While skill acquisition is the essential goal of the functional approach, the acquisition of knowledge is also valued, but only when it is directly applied as a life skill in a reality situation. A functional curriculum is appropriate for use in a special class or a special school. As an instructional method, it is of particular value to teachers of mainstreamed classes who must make functional adaptations to the traditional curriculum if facilitation of life skills is to be sought while teaching within the customary subject area format. These adaptations require teachers to examine the academic knowledge and skill competencies of the traditional curriculum and seek practical applications for each of the elements identified therein. The nature of each academic subject must be examined from a functional perspective in which knowledge for its own sake is eschewed and applications are assigned preeminence. Curriculum adaptations based on a functional approach do not result in a watered-down curriculum, as is often the case when students with learning and behavioral problems are taught. Rather, functional adaptations of traditional curricula will result in a vibrant, vital, and motivating curriculum, as academic content has been translated into meaningful applications. When a functional approach is employed, both mainstreamed students with disabilities and their nondisabled classmates are expected to develop the knowledge and skills that will increase the ability of all to meet the myriad demands of life with as much success and with as little stress as possible.

DEVELOPING A FUNCTIONAL CURRICULUM

In designing a functional curriculum, one must first arrive at a well-thought-out structure and format that captures the essence of the functional approach. The identification and analysis of the social roles that people play as children, adolescents, and adults can serve as the foundation for curriculum design (Bender & Valletutti, 1982; Valletutti & Bender, 1982). Closely allied to the concept of life skills, or functional curriculum, is the concept of social competence, or *adaptive behavior*. Adaptive behavior refers to the individual's effectiveness in meeting the standards and social demands of his or her environment based on one's age and the cultural group to which one belongs (Grossman, 1983). The goals of adaptive skills instruction generally fall into three categories: socialization, personal appearance, and recreation and leisure-time utilization.

Curricular models in the area of *career education* emphasize not only work careers, but have been expanded to include life career education which seeks to develop skills relevant to broad-ranging participation in the life of the total community. Career education involves a comprehensive educational program that starts early and continues into adulthood. Functional life skills identified as being appropriate for career education programs include: managing family finances; selecting, managing, and maintaining a home; caring for personal needs; raising children and family living; buying and preparing food; buying and caring for clothing; engaging in civic activities; using recreation and leisure; and mobility (Kokaska & Brolin, 1985). Clark (1979) has presented a school-based curricular model in career education that focuses instruction in four areas: values, attitudes, and habits; human relationships; occupational information; and acquisition of job and daily living skills. A career education model developed by Brolin (1986) is Life Centered Career Education (LCCE). This curriculum identifies 22 major competencies deemed necessary for persons to function effectively in school, family, and community roles. These skills are categorized into three major domains: daily living, personal/social, and occupational.

Developers of functional life skills, adaptive behavior, or career education curricula must identify and thoroughly examine the life situations that are faced by members of a particular society, and then specify the behaviors expected of society members as they function within that society at different stages of their life. While identified curriculum goals and objectives should be appropriate to the student's age and level of functioning, the long-range orientation of education requires that competencies needed by and expected of adults be given priority.

Functionally oriented curricula must have an adult outcomes emphasis. This is especially true for those students with disabilities and their nondisabled peers for whom a college education is neither appropriate nor desired. Adult-outcomes curricula have become less intensively focused on vocational training. These curricula deal more comprehensively with the numerous elements necessary for successful adult adjustment (Cronin & Gerber, 1982). Common foci include the development of consumer skills, home management and budgeting, civic and social responsibilities, and leisure skills. Students with learning and behavioral disabilities, as well as those students who have been identified in the past as slow learners and who have been experiencing long-term frustration and minimal success in school, are likely to be motivated by learning experiences that shift attention away from inadequate academic performance and toward the types of activities that are relevant to present and future needs. Regardless of their age or grade, students should be continuously provided with learning experiences designed to prepare them for their life after formal schooling.

If the social-role perspective rather than the traditional subject-area perspective is to be the determinant of the format, structure, and content of the functional curriculum, teachers and trainers must then decide which competencies, identified as goals and instructional objectives, should be included in the curriculum. As teachers and trainers themselves must fulfill various personal and social roles, their own lives can serve as curricular microcosms from which to identify desired learning outcomes. By examining their own lives and the lives of other adults, instructors may readily identify what life skills are needed by successfully functioning people. Additionally, students themselves, especially during the adolescent years, are excellent sources of functionally relevant instructional objectives (Polloway et al., 1989).

After analyzing the various life skills needed, teachers and trainers need to decide whether a particular skill warrants inclusion in a functional curriculum. *If a skill is needed or may be needed by individuals in a given society now or at sometime in the future, it belongs in the functional curriculum.* If a skill has little or no practical value then it should not be included. For example, instructional objectives—such as "the student will diagram the parts of a sentence," "the student will identify the subject and predicate," or, "the student will state the Pythagorean Theorem"—have no place in a functional curriculum. If the skill is a life skill that is useful *now* to a child or will be useful in the youngster's *future* as an adolescent and an adult, it belongs in the functional curriculum. Patton, Beirne-Smith, and Payne (1990) suggest that the selection of target functional behaviors should be governed by their adaptive potential, their direct and frequent application to the student's immediate environment, the likelihood of successful skill acquisition, the potential for improving the quality and level of services available to the student, and their impact on the reduction of dangerous or harmful behaviors.

Once the general functional curriculum has been developed, the student's individual education plan or individualized curriculum must then be formulated with critical attention paid to instructional priorities. Priorities are established, in part, by responses to the following questions:

1. Will acquisition of a designated prerequisite or developmental skill lead to the acquisition of an essential functional skill? For example, in a prelinguistic child, the stimulation of babbling has functional relevance even though on the surface it may at the time of instruction appear to have no direct application or functional value.

2. Is the skill to be developed of practical value *now* to the student as the youngster functions on a daily basis?

3. Will the skill to be acquired be needed by the student in the *future*? Certainly, a skill of immediate application must be assigned greater curricular priority than a skill to be applied in the future. Clearly, during the early years of schooling, instructors must provide learning experiences that deal with dressing and undressing skills (when needed) and leave the development of grooming skills related to shaving for later instruction.

4. Has the student demonstrated an actual need for the development of a particular skill? For example, if the teacher or trainer observes that a student is experiencing difficulty in exiting from the classroom because the child is unable to turn

the doorknob, then this particular skill should be assigned priority status.

5. Has the student expressed the desire to acquire a specific skill? Students often will communicate their programming needs to teachers. For example, a student may say, "I wish I could tie my shoes by myself so my brother will stop making fun of me!"

6. Do the parents believe that the acquisition of a particular skill will increase the student's adaptive behavior or performance in the home?

7. Will the student's acquisition of a specific skill improve the student's performance in school-related tasks? For example, "The student follows simple directions," for a particular student may become a priority functional skill for instructional purposes and for behavioral management.

8. Does the skill have survival value? Clearly teaching a student how to cross a street safely has greater priority than teaching the youngster to read for pleasure. The hope is that the student who possesses safety and health skills will survive to read for pleasure.

9. Will the development of a particular skill facilitate the acquisition of skills pertinent to the goals of other human service professionals who are providing the student with needed related services?

From the responses to these questions and with significant input from parents and relevant human service professionals, teachers and trainers must articulate the student's individual curriculum or program plan with identified instructional priorities. Individualized instructional priorities are established to determine program sequences and program emphases.

FUNCTIONALITY AS AN INSTRUCTIONAL PROCESS

To teach a functional objective in a functional way, teachers and trainers must ask the critical question, *"Under what life circumstances is this functional skill applied?"* The answer to this question then shapes the functional learning experience or lesson. For example, if the instructional goal is, "The student verifies change received," the response to the question *"under what life circumstances?"* may be "when making a purchase" or "when paying the check at a restaurant." Logically, a lesson then would follow, taking place either in a restaurant or in a simulated setting in the classroom. For example, a peer could be assigned to play the part of a waiter who passes out menus, takes the meal order, serves the meal, gives the student the bill, and then gives incorrect change. The student, in this functional lesson, is expected to play the part of a "wise" customer who determines that the change received is incorrect and asks for the correct change.

A recent example of a teacher's failure to ask the key question *"under what life circumstances?"* occurred during a college supervisor's observation of a student teacher's lesson. The student teacher had indicated in her plan that she was teaching the functional objective, "The students will identify the parts of their body." The student teacher, however, utilized a conventional approach in teaching this functional objective. She pointed to the various parts of a skeleton, while asking the students to name the parts to which she pointed.

If the student teacher, however, had asked the relevant question, she would have realized that most people (except, perhaps, medical students) are never, in this world, going to be required to identify the bones on a skeleton. Students, however, do need to identify their body parts, as for example, when indicating to parents and physicians where they are experiencing pain or where they have been injured. A functional lesson based on the functional objective of naming body parts then might involve a role play in which students play the part of visitors to a clinic, hospital, or private doctor's office setting in which they must describe their symptoms and relevant events leading up to their injury or pain. In this way, naming the body parts is applied to and practiced in a reality-based situation. A functional scenario such as this is meant to capture the essence of a real life situation.

A second experience, involving a teacher who was convinced that she was teaching from a functional perspective, further illustrates the failure to fully understand the nature of the functional method. A teacher of children with moderate-to-severe intellectual restrictions, wishing to demonstrate the progress being made by her students to her college supervisor, asked her class to line up. She then proceeded to give each student the following directions: "Turn on the cold water, then the hot water, and make the water warm." The teacher was indeed pleased by the students' demonstration of the functional skills of: identifying the water faucets by the letter imprints, "C" and "H," following a sequence, carrying out the motor task, and tempering the water. Unfortunately, she did not realize that she was also teaching the students to waste water. To make the lesson truly functional the water that each of the students drew from the sink should have been *used* for a purpose such as washing vegetables for a healthy mid-morning snack, washing their hands before eating lunch, and drawing water to irrigate the classroom plants.

Once the functional circumstances have been identified, teachers and trainers must arrange for a learning experience replication in the real setting, if possible—whether it is applied in the home, school, or community. Parents and other caregivers must be helped to understand how to assist students in carrying out functional "homework" assignments such as: storing food, household appliances, cleaners and cleansers, utensils, clothing, and linens in appropriate places. Teachers, on the other hand, must assume major responsibility for such school-related skills as working cooperatively with peers to complete a work assignment. Both parents and teachers must assume shared responsibility for providing educational experiences in community settings.

If the reality setting is not available or practical, functional learning experiences should be provided in classroom simulations designed to develop home and community-related skills. To accomplish this, the school must be suitably equipped with home-like furniture, decorations, appliances, and materials (cleaners, vacuums, mops, stoves, refrigerators, beds, and lamps). To simulate the community, the school may house an in-school supermarket, an in-school bank, in-school work sites, an in-school flea market, and an in-school bookstore.

THE SCOPE OF THE FUNCTIONAL CURRICULUM

As a functional curriculum is skill-oriented and relevant to the daily behaviors required and expected of people, it is most beneficial to organize it in terms of the various roles people play in life. Included among these roles are the following:

The person as:

1.   A responsible individual who functions as independently and as successful as possible—cognitively, physically, and emotionally;
2.   A socially skilled individual who engages in effective interpersonal and social behaviors and who works cooperatively with others for mutually agreed upon goals and for the benefit of society in general;
3.   A student who learns from others and, as a tutor, helps others to learn;
4.   A member of a family unit; first as a *child* (with a well-defined role and responsibilities) in a family unit living in the same household with a mother, father, brother (older and younger), sister (older and younger), grandparents, and even household workers such as a housekeeper; then as a *child* in relationship to family members living outside the home, for example, uncles, aunts, and cousins

then as an *adolescent*; and, finally as an *adult* in the family unit who assumes the various roles of spouse, parent, and the son or daughter of aging parents;

5. A member of his or her own personal community—that is, as a neighbor and friend;
6. A member of the larger community who is a responsible and responsive citizen of that community;
7. A consumer of goods and services and participant in diverse financial transactions;
8. A producer of goods or services—that is, as a worker;
9. A participant in diverse leisure-time activities;
10. A traveler who moves about the community while fulfilling all other social roles.

THE TRADITIONAL CURRICULUM AND ITS FUNCTIONAL ADAPTATIONS

"Adaptive skills are necessary to decrease an individual's dependence on others and increase opportunities for school and community participation" (Drew, Logan, & Hardman, 1992, p. 257). A functional approach to teaching academic skills is consistent with a philosophical orientation in which teachers and trainers have as their overriding goal the adaptation of the individual student to society (Lerner, 1989).

If educators look at the development of adaptive skills from a career education perspective, then it is imperative that they infuse career education concepts into the content of the regular curriculum. Lamkin (1980), in describing career education, states that it "brings meaningfulness to the learning and practice of basic academic skills by demonstrating to students and teachers alike the multitude of ways in which these skills are applied in work and daily living. A career education emphasis brings observable, experiential relevance to social studies, health, and science curricula, assisting students in perceiving the relationship between educational subject matter and the larger world outside the classroom" (p. 71).

A functional curriculum is an adaptive learning and a career education curriculum. In this approach to instruction, the basic academic skills are taught in the context of daily living activities. Browder and Snell (1987) have stressed that when attempting to functionalize learned skills, the teacher must use instructional materials that are realistic. Traditional materials are not practical because the student is unable to relate the materials to his or her world. Valletutti and Bender (1982) point out that, "a traditional way of teaching color concepts is to introduce young children to various colored shapes, beads, and blocks. A functional approach, on the other hand, would involve the learner with objects he or she will come into contact with while functioning in real-life situations and activities" (p. 2). They continue by citing such life situations as coordinating various articles of clothing, identifying fruit, locating color-coded seats in a sports stadium, identifying tropical fish in a home aquarium, and playing table games that have color-coded markers and pathways.

Teaching functional skills within the context of the traditional subject areas requires identifying student-based competencies from an adult-outcome perspective. The following areas of the traditional curriculum may be accommodated to meet the requirements of the functional curriculum.

The Language Arts

Student behaviors in oral and written language comprehension (listening and reading) are identified in Chapter 5. Functional approaches to the development of speech and writing skills follow.

Speech

The ultimate goal for speech instruction is, "The student will speak intelligibly with the articulation, syntactical, semantic, and vocal patterns typically found in adults" (Valletutti & Bender, 1985, p. 131). When this goal is viewed from a functional orientation, it may be organized according to the following structure:

A. General Communication

1. The student communicates personal information—that is: birthplace; present address; number of siblings; number, ages, and sex of children; occupation; interests; and hobbies.
2. The student engages in informal interpersonal communication as in simple conversations in a variety of settings; for example, at a party, on a work break, at a picnic, or at a restaurant. Topics (depending on age, sex, and cultural backgrounds of the participants) might include the weather, clothing, sports, food, the media and media stars, current events, restaurants, hobbies, and members of the opposite sex.
3. The student gives instructions and directions, as in telling someone how to get to one's home or telling someone how to perform a specific task.
4. The student tells anecdotes, stories, and jokes to others in informal conversations, whether face-to-face or over the telephone.

B. Dating and Courtship Talk

   1. The student asks for a date in the proper manner.
   2. The student engages in conversations appropriate to a courtship and loving relationship.

C. Formal Communication

   1. The student participates successfully in job interviews in which the individual must "sell" him- or herself to prospective employers.
   2. The student communicates as a subordinate to a supervisor as in: student to teacher, child to parent, worker to supervisor.
   3. The student communicates in a serious or important situation as in discussing symptoms with a physician, exploring psychosocial problems with a therapist, sharing sexual needs with a mate, discussing religious and moral issues with a member of the clergy, and asking one's boss for a raise.
   4. The student converses about serious topics such as politics, religion, sex, and other issues of a controversial, highly emotional, or serious nature.
   5. The student makes a presentation or a speech to a group; for example, trying to convince a community group to organize and advocate in order to avoid the destruction of an historic landmark.

D. Speaking for Pleasure

   1. The student reads aloud a prose or poetry selection to a friend, mate, or child, desiring to share the pleasure of the sound pattern and the content.
   2. The student tells anecdotes, stories, and jokes in interpersonal interactions.
   3. The student sings alone, as part of a group, or as a member of a chorus or choir.
   4. The student engages in chanting, singing, and speaking during ceremonial occasions such as religious services.
   5. The student participates in creative dramatics and other improvisations and acts in formal play productions.

Writing

   1. The student writes personal data on applications and other forms and blanks.
   2. The student writes simple notes and messages.
   3. The student writes lists to organize his or her behavior, for example, shopping and packing lists.

4. The student writes cards and personal letters.
5. The student writes business letters, including letters of complaint and letters of inquiry.
6. The student writes creatively.

Arithmetic

1. The student identifies and writes numerals used in personal data; for example, his or her birth date, address, and social security number.
2. The student identifies numerals as they appear in the community on transportation vehicles, buildings and homes, elevators, and other locations.
3. The student carries out various transactions involving money.
4. The student uses measuring devices and carries out diverse operations involving enumeration and measurement.
5. The student behaves as a skilled consumer of goods and services and as a successful participant in financial transactions.

Science and Health

1. The student behaves in ways that prevent illness and injury.
2. The student follows prescribed treatment procedures when ill or injured.
3. The student carries out simple first aid procedures.
4. The student behaves as responsibly as possible in using medicines, vitamins, and minerals and refrains from using drugs.
5. The student behaves responsibly in relation to the use of alcohol, nicotine, and caffeine.
6. The student functions as a responsible sexual being, behaving in ways that will bring him or her acceptance, love, and pleasure.
7. The student cares for and raises pets.
8. The student cares for and raises plants.
9. The student goes for nature walks and hikes.
10. The student collects natural objects for collections and arts and crafts projects.
11. The student uses tools and equipment to perform various motor tasks.
12. The student safely handles and operates electrical appliances, machinery, and apparatus.
13. The student safely uses ventilation, heating, and air conditioning equipment.
14. The student safely uses household cleaners and chemicals.

15. The student safely uses grooming materials.
16. The student prepares food.

Social Studies

1. The student identifies available natural environmental recreation and leisure sites.
2. The student identifies possible locations for vacations and other travel opportunities.
3. The student behaves as a wise consumer of goods and services and engages successfully in financial transactions.
4. The student exercises his or her right to vote and otherwise engages in political processes.
5. The student describes the nature, role, and function of the judicial and criminal justice system.
6. The student identifies and uses governmental and other social and human service agencies to meet his or her needs.
7. The student identifies and uses those governmental and private recreational and cultural institutions that will enrich his or her life.
8. The student participates in the activities of diverse cultural groups and appreciates their distinct contribution to American and world culture.
9. The students acquire insights into human behavior from an understanding of the historical interactions between human nature and events.

SUMMARY

This chapter has defined the functional approach, described how to develop a functional curriculum, discussed how to teach functionally, explicated the scope of the functional curriculum, and provided insights into how to teach functionally when constrained by a curriculum that is structured by traditional subject areas. The various terminologies used in the literature that deal with the functional approach to teaching have been noted: life skills curricula, adult-outcomes curricula, career education, adaptive behavior skills development have all been identified as being synonymous with functional learning.

Teachers of students with disabilities and teachers of nondisabled students should realize that it is easy to make functional adaptations to traditional curricula. Many teachers and parents resist a functional approach because of their own experiences as students who were taught from a traditional perspective. Teachers also may resist this approach because of the nature of teacher preparation programs they experienced. With the passage of time and with student progress, most parents and teachers of students with disabilities will become convinced of the extraordinary power of a functional approach to: motivate, interest, and excite students; to build self-esteem; to significantly increase student achievement; and primarily to help students adapt to life's demands and challenges and thus live a life that brings more success, happiness, and pleasure than would have the old traditional curricula and traditional instructional methods.

The authors have developed the following "Functional Perspective Questionnaire" which they use as a pre- and posttest assessment of the perceptions of preservice and inservice teachers in relation to the functional approach to instruction.

A Functional Perspective Questionnaire

Directions: For each of the items below, circle the letter or letters of those instructional objectives that are written from a functional perspective. Remember, there may be *more than one* correct answer.

1.   a.   The student will name the seasons.

b.   The student will dress appropriately to the season and weather conditions.

c.   The student will purchase fruits and vegetables during traditional growing seasons when likely to be of superior quality and lower in price.

d.   The student will participate in recreational activities according to seasonal climate differences.

2.   a.   The student will fill in the days on a blank wall calendar.

b.   The student will write their appointments on a wall calendar or in a personal calendar.

c.   The student will write the birthdays of family members and close friends on a wall calendar or in a personal calendar.

d.   The student will discuss the origins of the names of the days of the week.

3. a. The student will draw a picture of a goat, boat, and a coat as part of his or her phonetic skill development.

    b. The student will draw a map of his or her school building to locate such elements as emergency exits, the nurse's office, and the auditorium.

    c. The student will draw a picture illustrating an aspect of his or her summer vacation.

    d. The student will draw pictures of at least two animals classified as ungulates.

4. a. The student will follow the directions appearing on bottles of personal medicine.

    b. The student will identify the numbers and destinations of public busses.

    c. The student will read the stories found in his or her basal reader.

    d. The student will read the *Driver's Manual*.

5. a. The student will describe his or her symptoms when feeling ill.

    b. The student will use language courtesies such as: "Please!" and "Excuse Me!"

    c. The student will recite the "Gettysburg Address" from memory.

    d. The student will name the cranial nerves in order.

6. a. The student will identify the price of admission at theaters and sports arenas.

    b. The student will multiply four-place numbers by three-place multipliers.

    c. The student will add the unlike fractions: $\frac{3}{13}$, $\frac{5}{27}$, and $\frac{9}{84}$.

    d. The student will identify equilateral, right, and isosceles triangles.

7. a. The student will name all the basic food groups.

    b. The student will prepare a weekly menu of nutritious foods.

    c. The student will name common childhood diseases.

    d. The student will identify steps he or she can take to prevent illness and injury.

8. a. The student will raise and care for pets and plants.
    b. The student will name the various breeds of dogs.
    c. The student will grow a vegetable garden.
    d. The student will make a chart of the vitamins and minerals found in fruit and vegetables.

9. a. The student will identify the chemical composition of water and salt.
    b. The student will use chemical substances safely.
    c. The student will store cleaners and chemicals in safe places.
    d. The student will solve chemical equations.

10. a. The student will use electrical appliances in a safe manner.
    b. The student will identify the contributions made by: Watts, Volta, and Ampere.
    c. The student will change a burned-out light bulb.
    d. The student will define the terms: magma, lava, dormant, and extinct.

11. a. The student will appropriately use the numbers and letters appearing on the operating panel of a self-service elevator.
    b. The student will locate the correct seat in a theater or stadium from reading his or her admission ticket.
    c. The student will say the letters of the alphabet in order.
    d. The student will copy the letters from an alphabet chart.

12. a. The student will describe how tornadoes are formed.
    b. The student will seek appropriate shelter when there is a tornado warning.
    c. The student will discuss the differences among a tornado, cyclone, monsoon, and hurricane.
    d. The student will store food and water in case of an emergency.

13. a. The student will discuss ways to avoid and settle disagreements.
    b. The student will discuss the causes of the Civil War.
    c. The student will discuss the celebration of the first Thanksgiving and the reasons why people still have celebrations today.
    d. The student will discuss the importance of the following dates: 1066, 1492, and 1776.

14. a. The student will identify agencies in the community where he or she can go for help in time of need.

   b. The student will participate in community clean-up campaigns.

   c. The student will locate the place where he or she may vote.

   d. The student will discuss the key events in the settlement of his or her community.

15. a. The student will behave in ways that will assist him or her in acquiring and maintaining friendships.

   b. The student will identify famous friends in history, such as Damon and Pythias.

   c. The student will behave in ways that make him or her a good neighbor.

   d. The student will avoid being exploited by "friends."

16. a. The student will describe supply-side economics.

   b. The student will prepare a weekly budget.

   c. The student will complete a W2 form.

   d. The student will define the term "laissez-faire."

17. a. The student will register to vote.

   b. The student will name the three branches of government.

   c. The student will name the last three presidents in order.

   d. The student will identify behaviors that are against the law and might get him or her into trouble.

18. a. The student will correctly spell the words in his or her spelling book.

   b. The student will correctly spell (or at least so that he or she can recognize the item) the items on his or her shopping list.

   c. The student will correctly spell the information he or she has written on an invitation to a party at his or her home.

   d. The student will select the correctly spelled word from a list in which the other words are misspelled.

19. a. The student will identify by color and other clues food that is spoiled.

   b. The student will purchase clothing for the purpose of having color-coordinated outfits.

   c. The student will string wooden beads according to a teacher's model.

   d. The student will name the primary colors.

20. a. The student will adjust his or her clothing after toileting.

   b. The student will go to the appropriate sex-designated public bathrooms.

   c. The student will clean him- or herself properly after toileting.

   d. The student will practice turning the water faucets on and off in the bathroom.

Answer Key: 1. b, c, d 2. b, c 3. b 4. a, b, d 5. a, b 6. a
7. b, d 8. a, c 9. b, c 10. a, c 11. a, b 12. b, d
13. a, c 14. a, b, c 15. a, c, d 16. b, c 17. a, d
18. b, c 19. a, b 20. a, b, c

3

INFORMAL EDUCATIONAL ASSESSMENT AND INSTRUCTIONAL PLANNING

W hen facilitating the cognitive development of students with disabilities from a functional perspective, it is particularly appropriate that teachers and trainers use informal rather than formal assessment techniques and devices. A variety of informal assessment strategies are available for instructors to assist in designing and implementing individualized educational plans and individualized transition plans which focus on specific life skills. These are assessed as students perform activities when using real-life materials, in real-life situations, and, whenever possible, in actual settings. This chapter explores the nature, role, and scope of informal assessment as it relates to the instructional process.

INFORMAL ASSESSMENT

Informal assessment is essentially used in planning instruction and in evaluating student progress toward identified instructional goals and objectives. On the other hand, formal assessment involves the administration of standardized, norm-referenced tests for the primary purpose of identification, classification, or diagnosis (Mercer, 1991). While assessment has a number of goals including, screening, referral, classification, and the evaluation of instruction, the role of informal assessment as it relates to the instructional process is the subject of this chapter. *The purpose of assessment is to improve instruction.* According to Christenson and Ysseldyke (1989), the primary purpose of assessment activities is not to focus on prediction but to design appropriate instructional interventions. Bersoff (1973) states, "The purpose of assessment should be specified first. . . . The only legitimate reason for spending time . . . is to generate propositions which are useful in forming decisions to benefit persons under study. . . . Within that definitional framework . . . tests are generally not helpful in the acquisition of relevant knowledge to the accurate identification of potential talent nor the construction of intervention strategies for those assessed" (p. 893).

Mercer (1991) cites the principal advantages and disadvantages of informal assessment. "they 1. Can be constructed easily from graded curriculum materials and/or scope and sequence skills lists. 2. Might reduce the student's tension and anxiety. . . . 3. Can be devised and administered by the teacher. . . . 4. Can be given by the person who is in the best position to observe the student in a variety of situations. 5. Can be used to evaluate the validity of formal tests. 6. May be given frequently and focus on any area" (p. 145). He continues by pointing out some of the disadvantages of informal tests, including the fact that they are time-consuming to develop, require knowledge about the sequence of skills to be tested, and necessitate substantial clinical judgment and thus are subject to examiner bias.

Informal assessment methods are similar to formal methods—differing, however, in that they seek relevant information about students under less rigorous conditions. While informal assessment lacks the normative data of more formal methods, it is more relevant to instruction (Patton et al., 1990). Overton (1992) states that, "Informal assessment is used everyday . . . [it] includes worksheets, written samples of the student's work, teacher-made tests and quizzes, oral reading assignments, oral responses, group projects, and class assignments" (p. 5). He further suggests, "Many other informal assessment methods are used in monitoring the academic progress of students. Some of these methods combine the techniques of error analysis, direct measurement, CBA [curriculum-based assessment], probes, and criterion-referenced testing. These methods include teacher-made checklists, work samples, permanent product recording, and questionnaires" (p. 249). Stiggins (1985) has indicated that teachers require assessment data obtained from assessment materials and procedures they develop themselves for the purpose of accumulating instructional insights from a constantly changing and dynamic classroom.

Whenever a test is directly tied to the curriculum, it becomes a curriculum-based assessment (CBA) device (Overton, 1992). CBA is a systematic procedure for determining the educational needs of students. It is based on their performance relevant to the school's general curriculum and the student's individualized instructional goals and objectives. Specific test items are formulated directly from the material to be taught (Bender & Valletutti, 1985). There are two specific forms of CBA: precision teaching and mastery teaching. In precision teaching, an educational task is analyzed into its pattern and hierarchy of skills, while in mastery teaching, the smaller parts of the instructional task are assessed. CBA can assist in focusing the teacher's attention on changes in student behavior, thus enhancing the relationship between assessment and teaching (Deno & Fuchs, 1987).

A frequently used in-class method of informal assessment is criterion-referenced testing (CRT), in which instructors measure the student's skills in relation to assigned mastery levels (Patton et al., 1990; Salvia & Ysseldyke, 1988). Criterion-referenced assessment (CRA) compares the performance of a student to a given criterion, such as a curricular objective, rather than to a norm group. Teachers and trainers may not use only standardized CRTs, they may develop their own CRTs, that will assist them in instructional planning by directly linking assessment to the school's or the student's individualized curriculum. CRTs measure a student's mastery of specific skills. Two critical elements in the formulation of CRTs are the identification of its contents and the establishment of a desired level of performance or mastery for the specific content to be mastered (Ysseldyke, Algozzine, & Thurlow, 1992). Another approach to CRT is the use of judgment-based assessment (JBA), in which teachers and trainers incorporate the observations and insights of parents and other caregivers into their instructional planning decisions (Patton et al., 1990).

Curriculum-based assessment, criterion-referenced testing, judgment-based assessment, and the use of worksheets, samples of the student's work products, questionnaires, and teacher-made checklists, tests, and quizzes are all designed to lead to insightful planning and productive instruction.

INSTRUCTIONAL PLANNING

Teachers, as part of the instructional planning process, must be continuously aware of the need to devote class time to explorations of the student's interests, learning styles, and responses to alternate teaching strategies (Dunn, 1984). Lessons, therefore, must be planned and implemented for the specific purpose of assessment for instructional planning whenever there is a need to ascertain whether prerequisite or corequisite skills for specific instructional goals and objectives are present. Exploratory or assessment lessons investigate the student's skills, problems, and interests as well as assess his or her responses to different instructional approaches (clinical teaching). The roles of assessor, program planner, and program implementor are inextricably interwoven. Professional separation of these roles invariably leads to educational practices that are inappropriate, irrelevant, and illogical.

It is clear that a teacher's effectiveness as the principal participant in the initial design and in subsequent revisions of individualized education plans (IEPs) and individualized transition plans (ITPs) is dependent on his or her continuous involvement in the assessment process. Obviously, an IEP and an ITP must reflect the reality of the student's demonstrated performance in relation to desired or expected learning outcomes. Educational programming without a foundation in student assessment is patently counterproductive, as is educational assessment that does not result in the subsequent individualization of instruction.

It is also clear that the student needs to be evaluated in terms of the generally recognized goals of the school as articulated in the general curriculum and, when appropriate, in the curricula for designated student subpopulations—provided, of course, that these curricula have been designed to meet the diverse needs of students. Studies conducted by Collier (1988) and Ames and Ames (1984) support the position that special students should be treated as individuals within the context of the general curricular goals and objectives, provided that the criteria are rationally and realistically determined. Unfortunately, this is often not the case, as curriculum patterns and goals for learners with disabilities invariably remain fixated on and obsessed with traditional academic minutia and infrequently deal with the students' current and future functional needs. There is a pervasive disregard for the position that curriculum development should be shaped by desired instructional outcomes (outcomes-based education) rather than by a list of specific subject matter to be covered. The goals, objectives, and instructional elements articulated in the traditional, academically oriented curriculum continue to shape and set the pattern and direction for educational assessment and programming for both the nondisabled and the student with disabilities (Gickling & Thompson, 1985; Guerin & Maier, 1983).

The curriculum for special students, regardless of the severity of their disabling condition, should be developed and taught from a functional perspective that emphasizes those diverse skills required by people as they meet and adapt to the many challenges of living in an increasingly complex and demanding world (Valletutti & Bender, 1985). The IEP for the student with special needs must not be based solely on the skills and knowledge specified in the traditional curriculum, *but also* must address the goals and objectives of a functional curriculum (Bagnato, 1980).

The development of IEPs as mandated by federal and state laws for all students identified as having disabilities requires special and regular teachers to engage actively and continuously in the process of educational assessment. Special reference must be made to the identification of instructional goals and assessing student progress toward these goals (Gearheart & Gearheart, 1990; Hargrove & Poteet, 1984; McLoughlin & Lewis, 1990; Valletutti & Salpino, 1979).

It is not only a legal requirement, but it is essential that teachers and related service personnel who are charged with implementing an IEP participate in its development. Special educators must be involved in the assessment process, first to determine, in concert with the other members of an interdisciplinary team, whether they believe a student suspected of having an educational disability meets established eligibility criteria (Landerholm, 1990). Secondly, educators must assist other members of the interdisciplinary team in designing the initial IEP for a student who has been collectively identified as having educationally disabilities. Thirdly, teachers must engage in the educational assessment process as IEPs are periodically modified during the student's years of schooling. Finally, teachers, must realize that the assessment data of the IEP are invariably out-of-date because the student is a dynamically functioning being in a constantly changing classroom environment. Therefore, they must continuously involve themselves in the ongoing assessment and instructional planning processes as they interact with students. Continuous teacher/learner interactions can provide teachers with instructional insights into their students' abilities and educational needs which should then lead ultimately to logical and effective programming decisions (Salvia & Ysseldyke, 1988).

The ongoing nature of educational assessment is especially relevant since students are ever-changing as they interact with people and objects in their environment; as maturation takes place (except in the case of progressive degenerative diseases and when functionally destructive environmental conditions exist); and as they encounter and deal with planned and randomly occurring events of their lives. Hopefully, they will be making continuous progress cognitively, motorically, socially, and emotionally through planned, serendipitous, and incidental learning experiences. Ideally, in some cases, students will make such significant progress that they will no longer require special education services and programs of any kind and at any level. Unfortunately, at times, there will be other students who will experience regression as their disabling condition exacerbates or as they fail to make progress because of inaccurate assessment, insufficient remediation, inappropriate developmental programming, or inadequate instructional practices.

The primary professional responsibility for instructional planning belongs to educators and not to other human service professionals such as psychologists, especially when the psychologist's educational and experiential background is in clinical psychology. Ysseldyke et al. (1992) have decried the use and misuse of school psychologists, describing them as "psychometric robots." While educational psychologists are concerned with the nature of teaching, learning, and motivation, teachers, as the *implementors* of educational programs, must be intimately involved in their design. The widespread practice of many school systems in which IEPs are designed by *"this year's"* teacher and other members of the team for *"next year's"* teacher and other team members must also be questioned. If teachers are to respond logically, creatively, and with immediacy as their students progress or fail to progress in response to instruction, they should be the ones involved in the program's initial design. In their program planning and implementation function, teachers must be constantly alert to the need to focus on a specific skill or aspect of an educational task that is interfering with the student's acquisition of the skill and thus requires immediate attention and remediation (Schuster & Griffen, 1990). Whenever a student completes an instructional task or goal, the teacher may then proceed to an instructional objective that logically follows and builds on previous learning. Whenever a student, however, fails to achieve an instructional task, the teacher must determine which element(s) in the task are interfering with the student's acquisition of that particular skill; and, subsequently, engage in remedial techniques designed to overcome the demonstrated problem(s). Educational assessment thus is an ongoing professional activity as it suggests specific revisions in the student's educational program, individually oriented methodological approaches, and in the use of particular instructional resources.

As required by federal and state laws, IEPs must be based on the student's present functioning level or current level of performance. Unfortunately, many school systems respond to this legal mandate by simply reporting the student's scores obtained on group achievement tests that depict the student as he or she was at the time of testing and that cannot possibly describe students in all their many dimensions and facets.

To meet the intent of federal and state laws that mandate an appropriate education for all students with disabilities from birth through 21 years of age, an IEP must flow logically from a current-level-of-performance or present-levels-of-functioning statement that portrays the student as explicitly and as thoroughly as possible.

THE CURRENT-LEVEL-OF-PERFORMANCE STATEMENT

Both federal and state legislation require that each IEP contains a current-level-of-performance or present-levels-of-functioning statement. Additionally, as an integral part of educational assessment and student progress reports, a current-level-of-performance statement is of inestimable value, as, if it is done correctly, it should graphically portray the student in terms of the youngster's actual and current performance. It is the current-level-of-performance statement that gives meaning and focus to the IEP. It emphasizes the central role of informal assessment as the foundation from which IEPs are designed. It further emphasizes the quintessential role of student performance as the determinant of individually assigned annual goals and their accompanying specific short-term instructional objectives. Therefore, a current-level-of-performance statement is a narrative *portrait* of the student, delineating and vivifying that student's abilities, problems, interests, and educational needs.

In writing a current-level-of-performance statement a teacher or teachers are required to work collaboratively with other team members to "paint" a portrait of the student in narrative terms that captures the student's typical *and* current performance patterns so clearly that all those who read it will be able to "see" the student as a dynamically functioning individual in all the child's dimensions. The current-level-of-performance narrative should not contain evaluative statements, but should describe the student in terms of individual performance and not stereotypically from either his or her diagnostic label or from grade/age level scores on a standardized test battery. When writing a narrative of this kind, one must rely heavily on *informal* assessment strategies that are to be utilized by teachers as they respond to student performance in terms of both the processes employed and products created.

The five informal assessment questions described below are meant to assist in the writing of the current-level-of-performance statement and thus in the design of the completed IEP.

THE FIVE INFORMAL ASSESSMENT QUESTIONS

If the teacher or teachers responsible for evaluating student performance are to be insightful observers who separate educationally significant behaviors from educationally irrelevant ones, they will need an observational model. The five questions that follow attempt to provide such a model. They are meant to focus attention on student performance as it occurs in the classroom and in other structured learning environments. They are also meant to assist in the identification of specific instructional goals and objectives. The school generally provides teachers with a recommended curriculum from which diagnostically oriented teachers are expected to select specific individualized goals and objectives based on their analysis of student skills and deficits. The teacher selects those items from the general curriculum and any existing special curricula so they may design an IEP or ITP that addresses the educational needs of each student and that serves as the student's individualized curriculum.

The First Question

The first question to be addressed is the most important one diagnostically, as all subsequent questions make programming sense only if the first question is answered as thoroughly and explicitly as possible. Further, answers to subsequent questions have instructional relevance only when viewed from the perspective of the response to the first question. Explicitness of response requires the use of behavioral terms, so that others, including parents who are essential and legally mandated members of the interdisciplinary team, are thoroughly informed about and familiarized with the student's performance. A narrative report is a powerful "report card" as contrasted with the limited communicative effectiveness of the numbers, letters, and brief statements recorded on typical report cards. Behavioral terms are necessary so that readers may "see" the functioning student through the eyes and ears of the teacher who has observed the student critically and has recorded in an organized fashion those insightful observations that suggest what and how to teach the student.

The first question, however, is the most difficult to answer, not because it is esoteric or complex but because it is apparently antithetic to typical human response sets. These authors, as a case in point, have been engaged in a simple experiment that dramatically illustrates the predilection of teachers to view student performance initially from a negative perspective. Unfortunately, this common human response is diagnostically contraindicated and instructionally counterproductive. The exercise described below has been used in numerous teacher workshops and classes to introduce the first diagnostic question.

A sample of a hypothetical student's work product (either a written language sample or a page of arithmetic computation) is presented to the group with no other information provided. For example the following hypothetical student arithmetic paper is presented:

John Jones

1. 24	2. 625	3. 598	4. 284	5. 20.43
+72	×2	−49	−83	+7.48
96	1,250	559	201	27.91

After the teachers and teacher candidates have had sufficient time to review the sample, the following question is posed, "What do you see?" In the literally thousands of educators and teacher candidates who have participated in this exercise, the answer has *always* been the same. "Number three is wrong!" This apparently universal negative response set to student work creates a significant obstacle to effective educational assessment and programming. A fixation on demonstrated errors grievously interferes with the establishment of an instructional starting point from which progress is sought and from which any resulting progress can be measured. The central diagnostic question then should be:

1. *What skills, knowledge, interests, and concepts has the student demonstrated?*

The emphasis must be placed on *demonstrated* skills since the education of students should be grounded in student performance and should be skill- or action-oriented. It is also important to ascertain the student's knowledge, especially when the student's knowledge has been successfully translated into meaningful action. The knowledge that a toothbrush is to be used to brush one's teeth is an underlying and necessary dimension of the action of brushing one's teeth. The student's interests also need to be identified because they suggest *how* to teach the student, that is, what materials should be used and what alternate methods should be selected because they will most likely motivate learning. For example, if a student demonstrates interest during free play in moveable toys, then moveable toys such as cars and wheels might be used to gain the child's attention and excite the youngster's interest. A further example might be using a musical instrument as an instructional approach when working with a student who requires improved fine motor skills and who demonstrates delight in musical exploration and creation. The use of music to facilitate fine motor development might result in greater progress than employing an arts and crafts project or a vocational shop activity. It is also important to ascertain the concepts that a student has already learned. For example, if the student already has acquired the concept that shoes, socks, and pants are all examples of clothing, then instructional time should not be wasted on this already acquired concept but might rather be devoted to helping the student acquire new concepts that will contribute to the student's overall cognitive development.

Only through an understanding of what skills, knowledge, and concepts currently exist in the student's behavioral repertoire can judicious decisions be made as to *what* new skills, knowledge, and concepts should be taught. Moreover, teacher awareness of the presence of these competencies will more likely lead to their utilization in the development of new skills that arise naturally and developmentally from existing ones.

The Second Question

The second question deals with error analysis that uses the information from errors on work samples made by students as a means of assessment (Bachor, 1979). This question explores several areas: it examines demonstrated problems, explores identified problems in terms of their patterns, specifies the student's level of mastery if partial acquisition is present, and focuses on the establishment of programming priorities. In order to effectively analyze the problems demonstrated by the student, teachers must engage in the task analysis and error analysis process. These processes involve breaking down an educational task (or instructional objective) into its component subskills and substeps and then analyzing error patterns in performance of the task. The subskills are those competencies that the student must possess while the substeps are those subtasks that the student must master before the assigned task can be achieved (Valletutti & Salpino, 1979).

2a. *What problems or errors have been demonstrated by the student?*

This part of question two deals simply with a description of the problems demonstrated by the student in the youngster's interactions in the classroom and other environments. For example, "David has consistently picked up small objects such as toy cars, blocks, and crayons with his preferred hand, but because of fine motor problems he does not release them easily when attempting to pass them to a classmate." It is often best to describe a problem in concert with an existing or related skill because such an approach provides an instructional focus on a circumscribed aspect of the task while it simultaneously establishes a starting point for the program.

The second part of question two is concerned with an analysis of the nature of the identified problem.

2b. *Are there demonstrated patterns in the identified problems?*

One should attempt to discover patterns because the presence of response patterns may provide insights relevant to the establishment of instructional priorities. Consistency of error is one factor in the establishment of programming priorities. (See question 2d.) Consistency of a demonstrated problem points not only to the severity of the problem but also to the frequency of its expression. In addition to consistency, one should also determine whether the error itself provides unexpected or unanticipated insights into the student's skills. For example, Student A consistently makes spelling errors in his independent written work. An examination of the type of error made, however, indicates that he possesses satisfactory auditory discrimination skills because he misspells words where there is a lack of phoneme-grapheme correspondence ("captin" for "captain" and "bin" for "been"). Student B, on the other hand, demonstrates a different pattern in her written work. She demonstrates either a perceptual or perceptual-motor problem while simultaneously demonstrating visual memory for words that are spelled nonphonetically. She wrote "cabtain" for "captain" and "peen" for "been." An analysis of the pattern of errors provides the teacher of these students with key diagnostic information needed to design specific remedial approaches.

The third part of question number two seeks to provide a description of exhibited errors in terms of the student's level of mastery—that is, does the student, at some time and in some contexts, demonstrate partial acquisition of the skill.

2c. *While there is a demonstrated problem, is there partial mastery or acquisition of the skill at some time and in some contexts?*

This aspect of question number two is related to the establishment of instructional priorities. A key element in the setting of educational priorities is the student's level of mastery of a particular skill expressed in terms of partial performance. Usually, a skill that is partially mastered is more likely to be fully mastered in a shorter period of time than a skill for which there is little or no mastery. The reinforcement value of rapid success should be considered in establishing programming priorities because of the powerful motivating force of successful achievement.

The final element in this multipart question deals with the establishment of educational priorities.

2d. *What priorities do you recommend for developmental and remedial programming?*

The establishment of instructional priorities is a complex enterprise since it requires the balancing of a number of competing forces. Clearly, teaching a student to cross a street safely has greater priority than teaching the child how to read. Unfortunately, a clear-cut choice such as this is rarely the instructional issue. Consideration in identifying priorities must be given to factors such as the impact of the acquisition of a specified skill on the student's:

1. Health and Safety
2. Cognitive Development
3. Level of Independence or Autonomy
4. Self-Concept
5. Functioning in the Classroom
6. Functioning in the Home
7. Functioning in the Community
8. Motivational Level
9. Acquisition of Related Skills
10. Positive Evaluation by Peers and Adults
11. Emotional and Social Development
12. Motor Development

The Third and Fourth Questions

The third and fourth questions are interrelated and play a vital part in the writing of an educational assessment or current-level-of-performance statement because unanswered diagnostic questions frequently occur. Sometimes these unanswered questions require the attention of other human service professionals and, at other times, they require specially designed assessment lessons by the instructor.

   3. *What additional evaluative information is required from other related human service professionals?*

The teacher may wonder, for example, whether a particular student's frequent request for teacher repetition of oral directions suggests the possible presence of a hearing loss, as a feasible explanation for such a behavior is a hearing loss. Referral to an audiologist or otologist for audiometric testing is warranted as one step in determining etiology. The reason for the failure to follow oral directions may indicate that the treatment intervention of another professional, in addition to specific instructional interventions, is necessary.

Yet another step that may be taken to ensure that as much evaluative information as necessary is obtained might require referring a student for a neurological examination to determine whether existing spinal cord damage (as in the case of a student with spina bifida) will prevent the student from developing bladder control thus making instructional programming in this area a nonproductive and frustrating enterprise for both student and teacher.

4. *What additional information must be obtained in terms of your own interactions with the student?*

This question deals with unanswered inquiries that time constraints or student developmental levels have prevented the teacher from exploring at an earlier time. As a case in point, educational assessments may have to be submitted to the multidisciplinary team, because of legal timelines or because of report due dates, before the teacher feels secure (because of insufficient data) in describing a student's behavior. This is especially true when the behavior in question has never or has infrequently been manifested in the normal ebb and flow of classroom events. The teacher or teachers involved in compiling the educational evaluation report may need time to design exploratory lessons in which diagnostic information, rather than teaching, is the objective. For example, a teacher may need to discover the dimensions of a student's auditory discrimination skills (because of articulation and/or reading problems) and will need to conduct several classroom activities employing teacher-made or formal tests of auditory discrimination.

The Fifth Question

The final assessment question is a summation one that leads directly to programming recommendations. It is presented here in two distinct patterns. The first pattern deals with the initial IEP while the second pattern deals with revisions in the student's current IEP or the design of a new IEP for the next school year.

5. *Based on your responses to the preceding questions, what recommendations would you make for annual instructional goals and short-term instructional objectives for inclusion in the student's initial IEP?*

or

Based on your responses to the preceding questions, what recommendations would you make for updating the student's IEP or for designing next year's IEP?

Once these five questions have been answered as thoroughly as possible, the information obtained then must be submitted to team members and to parents in a form that is as free from educational jargon and that is as explicit as possible. In order to meet this professional requirement, a suitable format for this assessment and/or student progress report is necessary.

THE FORMAT FOR THE EDUCATIONAL ASSESSMENT OR STUDENT PROGRESS REPORT

The response to the first question should be the basis for the first paragraph of the report because of its importance and because of its impact on the rest of the narrative's content. Problems demonstrated by the student along with their patterns and the student's levels of acquisition/mastery should be articulated in the second paragraph. Responses to questions three and four might be included either in an optional third paragraph or added after the programming recommendations are enumerated. The final paragraph, written in outline form, should be devoted to teacher programming recommendations. A sample section of a report is presented to clarify the relationship between the five diagnostic questions and the evaluative narrative. Lastly, the report should be written in sections that correspond to the subject areas of the curriculum, based on the individual student's special educational needs. A sample section of an educational assessment or student progress report follows.

A SAMPLE SECTION (SELF-CARE) OF AN EDUCATIONAL ASSESSMENT OR STUDENT PROGRESS REPORT

Self-Care

David takes care of his toileting needs independently. He undresses himself when the clothing items contain buttons or can be easily slipped over his head. He eats independently with a spoon and fork when the food is solid or semisolid. Drinking from a cup or glass is accomplished without difficulty in swallowing and without spillage.

There are several problems demonstrated. As yet David does not tie or untie his shoes. There is a pattern evident in his general inability to tie simple knots in arts and crafts projects and in package wrapping activities. He evidences problems consistently in buttoning his shirt. Although he is able to button his shirt, he usually ends up with buttons aligned incorrectly. His fingernails are often dirty; however, on two recent days, he was observed, on his own volition, cleaning his nails with his assigned nail brush. He has difficulty at lunch time with eating soup, invariably spilling it on his clothing. While he brushes his teeth, he characteristically either neglects to rinse his mouth of toothpaste or swallows the rinse water. While he is able to carry out the motor task of washing his hands, he typically fails to wash his hands after toileting.

As yet there has been no opportunity to observe David's use of a knife and fork in cutting food as there has been no need for him to do so, based on the nature of the food served at school. In the future, an exploratory lesson will be arranged to evaluate his skill relevant to this self-care task. Further, despite his attention to personal hygiene, he has a rather unpleasant body odor. He has been referred to a physician to ascertain whether there might be a metabolic or other medical reason for this self-care problem.

Based on my observations during the past 30 days, the following annual goals and specific instructional objectives are suggested.

Annual Goal	1.	David will dress himself independently.
Instructional	1a.	David will untie his shoes independently
Objectives	1b.	David will tie his shoes independently.
	1c.	David will button his shirt correctly.
	1d.	David will zip and unzip the fly of his pants independently.
	1e.	David will zip and unzip the zipper on his winter jacket independently.
Annual Goal	2.	David will wash his hands when appropriate.
Instructional	2a.	David will clean his nails when they are dirty.
Objectives	2b.	David will wash his hands after toileting.
	2c.	David will wash his hands after painting and other classroom projects in which his hands are likely to be soiled.
Annual Goal	3.	David will feed himself independently.
Instructional	3a.	David will eat soup without any spillage.
Objectives	3b.	David will eat ice cream and other easily spilled food without spillage or soiling his clothing.
Annual Goal	4.	David will brush his teeth independently.
Instructional	4a.	David will rinse his mouth after brushing his teeth.
Objectives		
	4b.	David will spit out the rinse water and then wash out the sink after brushing his teeth.

The sample section of an educational assessment or student progress report was provided to illustrate the relationship of the current-level-of-performance narrative to the formulation of annual goals and their short-term instructional objectives. This sample was composed from a functional perspective that deals with areas of student behavior rather than the traditional academic curricular focus. Many teachers and trainers must develop IEPs, however, from a traditional subject-matter focus.

Informal Assessment of Basic Academic Subjects

In order to respond fully to the five informal assessment questions, teachers and trainers must record, on a daily basis, their observations of student performance and their resultant instructional insights. In addition, they must organize classroom experiences that informally assess student knowledge, skills, and concepts. A discussion of possible informal approaches as they relate to the basic academic areas follows.

Speech

One way of obtaining a good sample of a student's speech is to prepare a series of high interest situational pictures and then ask the student to respond to the pictures by describing what he or she sees in them. A 10- to 15-minute sample obtained and recorded on high fidelity equipment in a quiet location should later be analyzed for skills and demonstrated problems. It should be recognized that this is one sample taken at one particular moment in time. Therefore, teachers should be cautious in making judgments and programming decisions based on this single sample. The sophisticated assessor, relying on clinical judgment from informal assessments, appreciates the conditional and subjunctive elements of the language and uses phrases such as, "It would appear from this sample that. . . ." "On the basis of this limited sample, one wonders whether. . . ." "It would seem from this one sample that the most critical area to concentrate on is probably. . . ." These equivocations are not meant to support a fence straddling approach but are meant to emphasize that judgments based on limited samples are, in reality, hypotheses that must then be supported by additional assessment data (Valletutti & Salpino, 1979).

A speech sample may be analyzed along two dimensions: the mechanics of oral communication and the structure of oral communication. The mechanics may be analyzed in terms of the following variables: articulation, voice production, fluency, pronunciation, and the visual components of the speech act. The structure of oral communication may be analyzed in terms of the following variables: word usage; grammatical usage; number of words; words per minute; number of communication units; mean length of communication units; vocabulary diversity; structural patterns; and index of subordinate clauses, phrases, modifiers, multiples, and compound structures used as expansion strategies (Valletutti & Salpino, 1979).

Reading

Howell and Morehead (1987) suggest several informal methods of assessing reading comprehension. Included in their recommendations are: following the youngster's reading of a story, asking the student questions concerning story details, including the sequence of events and the main idea; requesting the student to restate the story in the child's own words; asking the student to retell the story, using the same words used in the story; and employing the cloze method in which the student is asked to read a passage with missing words that the youngster must supply based on the context. Polloway et al. (1989) have described the intervention assessment approach to reading comprehension assessment in which the instructor asks him- or herself the following questions: "1. Does the student have relevant prior knowledge? 2. Does the student use that knowledge to make logical predictions about the selection? 3. Is the student able to set purposes for reading by formulating appropriate questions in preparation for reading? 4. When prior knowledge related to specific content is lacking, is the student able to use knowledge about the ways authors organize information to make logical predictions about passage content?" (p. 214). Decoding skills as well as speech and voice production problems may be assessed naturally while the student is reading aloud or by recording the student reading a selection aloud and then comparing the oral reading to the original text. In carrying out the analysis, it is best if teachers have previously developed a notation system for recording deviations from the original text. Errors to be noted include: addition of words; addition of a sound or word part; omission of a sound, word, or word part; substitution of a sound, word part, or word; ignoring of punctuation; errors in pronunciation; sound distortions; hesitations; and self-corrections (Mercer, 1991; Valletutti & Salpino, 1979). Mercer (1991) also recommends a miscue analysis in which errors are analyzed according to the following classifications: semantic—dealing with errors in meaning; syntactic—dealing with incorrect use of parts of speech; and graphic—dealing with errors in use of the wrong graphic representations. Graded word lists may be used to examine the student's word recognition skills and in determining a student's sight vocabulary, fluency level, and word attack skills in response to unknown words. Fluency level may be assessed by timing the student as he or she reads aloud and then by noting whether the youngster reads word-by-word or by phrases (Reid, 1988). Wixson, Bosky, Yochum, and Alvermann (1984) conducted metacognition interviews of students to ascertain their use of reading strategies. Their interview contained 15 open-ended questions that investigated the students' perception of the goal of the reading activity, their understanding of task requirements, and the strategies they used.

Writing and Spelling

The best way of analyzing written language and spelling skills and error patterns is through the collection and analysis of the student's written products. Assessment is then directed to the student's use of written language elements including mechanics (punctuation, grammatical usage, vocabulary diversity, sentence and paragraph structure, and spelling) and content, including fluency, theme, and plot. Fluency refers to the quantity of writing and is measured by a word-per-sentence analysis. Sentence type and form are measured by analyzing the type of sentence (simple, compound, and complex) and form is measured by the use of interrogative, declarative, imperative, and exclamatory sentences. Vocabulary diversity is measured by a type-token measure, stated as a ratio of the number of different words per hundred word segment supplemented by an index of unusual words used. Polloway and Smith (1992) recommend that ideation be assessed by asking the following questions, "1. Is the composition *relevant* to the topic assigned or selected. . . ? 2. Do the ideas . . . represent *original* thinking . . . ? 3. Does the composition demonstrate expression of *personal perspectives* . . . ? 4. Do the ideas expressed show a *clarity of thought*, presenting the major facets of a topic in appropriate sequence? 5. Does the composition reflect a *basic interest* in the topic, and thus a *motivation* to commit ideas to the written form?" (p. 392). Spelling samples can be obtained from dictated tests, free writing and compositions, responses to written questions in various content areas, and diverse seatwork assignments (Polloway & Smith, 1992).

Mathematics

According to Overton (1992) teachers may use CBA in combination with task analysis and error analysis to measure all areas of mathematics. Howell and Morehead (1987) suggest a number of methods for informally assessing math skills including: administering a basic facts test and asking the student to respond orally and giving a writing or copying digits test. Polloway et al. (1989) recommend that mathematics be assessed through: direct observation of a student's performance, interviews, checklists and rating scales, and an examination of the student's previous work and cumulative folder. Valletutti and Salpino (1979) suggest the development of a teacher-made inventory of math skills. They recommend that teachers and trainers: organize knowledge and skills into levels of difficulty, analyze relationships between mode of item presentation and student mode of response, and explore in depth the sequence and scope of the content area.

Cognitive Processes

According to Swanson and Watson (1982) cognitive process assessment is "embedded within Piaget's developmental theory of intelligence. . . . Specific tests can be developed to ascertain developmental milestones. The examiner may assess the child by using observation and task manipulation to get the child to answer several questions" (p. 162). They suggest such questions as: "Can the child consider the point of view of others?" "Does the child have a mental representation of a sequential series of actions?" "Can the child see that objects with common features form a class of objects?" and "Does the child have the ability to arrange objects according to some quantified dimension?" (p. 162). Assessment of a student's language base focuses on language acquisition, information processing mechanisms, conceptual process development, inductive processes, and semantic memory. Metacognition can be assessed at four levels: the student's perception of an individual's capabilities vis-a-vis a specific task, task variables that influence performance, the identification of a strategy, and evaluation criteria (Swanson & Watson, 1982).

SUMMARY

The role of a teacher is multidimensional. During the early years of schooling, teachers are required to teach every subject. They must be able to work with heterogeneous groups of students from diverse personal and cultural backgrounds operating at various achievement and developmental levels. They must be program adapters and program implementors. They must select judiciously and construct creatively their own teacher-made instructional materials. They must organize the classroom so that it facilitates and contributes to learning, and they must manage and improve behavior. They must also integrate research findings into classroom practice.

The ability to use informal assessment effectively, however, is essential to program adaptation and implementation and for the development of individualized program plans. Five basic questions have been offered in an attempt to provide a conceptual framework for creating evaluative reports, including current-level-of-performance narratives. The responses to these questions should provide instructional insights into what is an appropriate special education for students with learning and behavioral problems in the most normal or least restrictive educational environment. Further, these reports or narratives are essential elements in facilitating communication between the school and the home and between educators and other human service providers. Special educators realize that the involvement of the family is a key element in the success of the instructional program. The family is of vital importance in reinforcing classroom learning experiences, in carrying out home-based instruction, and in providing necessary community-based instruction in concert with the school. As carryover agents who provide practice for newly emerging skills, family members play a critical role in skill acquisition. As continuing models of acceptable performance and as resource providers for their children, family members play an essential role in the total education of their children whether these children are disabled or not.

Finally, in terms of the debate over formal and informal assessment, perhaps, the pertinent questions raised by Ysseldyke et al. (1992) should constantly be kept in mind, "When we look at the magnitude of the assessment process, at the large numbers of tests administered to students, we repeatedly ask. 'Why?' Why is it that school personnel administer so many tests to make decisions about students? Is it because they learn so much about the students and how to teach them? . . . We think . . . that there is much evidence to indicate that assessors learn very little about students from the students' performance on standardized tests" (p. 177).

PART II

COGNITIVE LEARNING FROM A FUNCTIONAL PERSPECTIVE

This second section of the text deals with the cognitive domain and how various aspects of it can be taught from a functional perspective. The cognitive domain involves: knowledge, comprehension, application, analysis, synthesis, and evaluation (Bloom, 1956). These cognitive categories are discussed under two broad headings: (1) comprehension and (2) critical thinking, which involves application, analysis, synthesis, and evaluation. There is also a brief discussion on functional learning—that is, how these competencies can be developed utilizing a functional approach. For each of these cognitive categories, readers have been provided with model instructional plans that illustrate the functional approach to cognitive development. Instructional plans for the development of comprehension have been provided for the four levels of comprehension: literal, interpretative, critical, and creative.

In order for students to master these cognitive categories, they must be able to form concepts of what they are learning. These concepts may not be clear all at once, but however amorphous these concepts may appear at the beginning, gaining knowledge, recalling information, making applications, or dealing with the higher levels of cognition requires conceptualization. Prior to discussing the categories of the cognitive domain, therefore, a chapter is devoted to concept development. Language plays a crucial role in cognitive development, learning, and in problem solving. This section, therefore, also includes a chapter on oral and written language.

Each of the chapters in this section has three areas. The first area discusses a cognitive aspect or category. The second describes the functional approach to teaching that aspect or category. The third presents a detailed instructional plan illustrating how that particular cognitive aspect or category may be taught from a functional perspective.

4

BUILDING CONCEPTS

L anguage in all forms—oral, written, or sign—plays a crucial role in cognitive development and learning. It is through language that one codifies experiences. However, words are only labels. The ability to acquire knowledge, recall information, make applications, solve problems, and see things in relational terms is based on the ability to form and understand concepts. Another way of describing words is that they are like the outer shell of nuts. One must crack the nutshell in order to get to the kernel, that is, concept. Knowing a word or idea, therefore, means having an understanding of the concept or concepts associated with it. Teachers often complain that many students experience difficulty in mastering vocabulary and in developing the ability to comprehend. One of the most important reasons students encounter this problem is that they are taught to pronounce and memorize words (labels) without understanding the concepts they represent. Understanding and building concepts are essential to the development of every area of the cognitive domain and consequently to learning.

In helping students to learn through the development of all areas of the cognitive domain, it is important for teachers and trainers to understand what concepts are, the relationship between concepts and the labels that represent them, how concepts are built, the role of background experiences in concept building, and the importance of concepts in every type of learning. Concepts are crucial to learning because they form the building blocks upon which generalizations, principles, processes, and methods are built.

CONCEPTS DEFINED

There are several definitions of concepts. Zintz (1970) says, "Concepts are personalized meanings held by an individual" (p. 237). Woodruff (1961) believes concepts are: "Mental images of life accumulated from personal experiences with life itself" (p. 57). Billings (1929) says, "Concepts are cues to the proper understanding of the situations to which they apply. Thus, a concept is both a summary of meaning gleaned from past experience and a cue to the meaning of the present situation" (p. 243). Finally, Roe, Stoodt, and Burns (1991) say, "Concepts are products of experience; they are the abstracted and cognitively structured mental experiences acquired by individuals in the course of their lives. . . . Concepts are a mental filing system that enable [sic] a person to sort out and organize relationships among specific items and instances" (p. 26).

In the light of these definitions, experience is the essence, the raw material that one uses to build concepts. One can conclude, therefore, that students' ability to understand and form concepts is directly related to the quality of their background experiences. Since concept development is essential to learning, teachers and trainers must assess the level and relevance of students' background experiences before presenting them with specific concepts for the students to learn. If students do not have the background experiences with which to gain understanding of words and ideas, teachers must provide experiences directly or vicariously for students to grasp the concepts they represent. Many students, including those with learning problems, can pronounce words and memorize words and ideas that they do not comprehend. Many students require repeated experiences and frequent reinforcement in order to achieve mastery. Some concepts are more difficult to learn and require more time and explanation to ensure that students fully understand them. To know a word or understand an idea means that one has mastered the concept for which that word or idea stands.

According to Montague, Huntsberger, and Hoffman (1989), concepts can be broadly divided into two categories: abstractions dealing with concrete objects such as flower, book, chair, snow, or animal and abstractions dealing with conditions or processes such as beauty, love, cold, verb, democracy, conducting, or art. Those concepts that deal with processes or conditions are more difficult to teach because they have no concrete reference. Montague et al. (1989) suggest that concepts which derive from objects are developed by a classification process of identifying those crucial features that define an object. Concepts related to process are very abstract and are more difficult to teach as well as to learn. Teachers must be aware that the more complex a concept, the more related concepts must be understood in order to understand, remember, and use that concept. For example, consider the difference in conceptualizing the concept "sunlight" and the concept "photosynthesis." It is easier to form concepts of "sunlight" than to understand the process by which plants make food by using water and air in the presence of sunlight.

A definition of a concept consists of a set of attributes that describe the concept. This list of attributes, or characteristics, could not define any other concept. Although other concepts may have one or more similar attributes, they will not have all the same attributes. For example, a definition of the concept "shoes" would include the attribute "article of clothing that is worn on the feet, touches the ground, and protects the feet from many injuries." There are several "articles of clothing" such as hat, socks, gloves, dress, pants, shirt, stockings, belt, and scarf. According to the most recently mentioned authors, there are two kinds of attributes, a *variable* attribute and a *critical* attribute. If one describes "shoes" as "an article of clothing" one is using a *variable* attribute, because this attribute may be used to define other related concepts. A *critical* attribute, on the other hand, is one that differentiates an object or idea from other objects or ideas that may or may not have the same *variable* attribute. Therefore, the *critical* attribute, that is, the one that distinguishes it from all other articles of clothing, is "worn on the feet, touches the ground, and protects the feet from many injuries." Learning involves understanding the distinctive as well the critical features of objects and ideas. Critical attributes are often very difficult to teach, because they cannot be represented by anything concrete.

Teachers and trainers need to take special care to provide students with many direct and vicarious experiences to help them comprehend and learn concepts. Instructors must remember that the difficulty in comprehending concepts increases in direct proportion to the complexity or abstractness of the concept. The more abstract a concept is, the more difficulty students will experience in learning it. Merely giving students the definition of a concept will not enable most students to understand, store, and apply these concepts in their daily lives. Roe et al. (1991) suggest several reasons why merely defining a concept is an inadequate method of teaching students to build concepts. First, a short simple definition of a concept may not provide sufficient information for understanding that concept and a very long, complex definition may require the inclusion and understanding of related and equally complex definitions. A simple definition of a concept like "democracy" does not teach a student the concept. It is only after having many direct and indirect experiences with "democracy" that the student will begin to understand the concept "democracy." Second, many definitions are not very clear or precise, as is illustrated by the following examples:

commission—the act of doing or perpetrating;

inhibition—the checking, restraining, or blocking of a mental process, psychological reaction.

These definitions are accurate; however, they are of little or no use to an individual who does not know the meaning of these words. Third, definitions may not always be appropriate to the context in which the given concept is used. Students would therefore experience difficulty in choosing the right definition from among many definitions given in a dictionary or glossary. Fourth, definitions do not help learners apply concepts in everyday situations. This does not mean that definitions should never be used in teaching concepts. It is important to remember, however, that they are only one aspect of teaching students to understand and form concepts. Teachers and trainers should use a combination of activities and methods to assist students in learning concepts.

HOW CONCEPTS ARE BUILT

The process of building concepts entails grouping objects and ideas or experiences with similar characteristics in specific categories. Concepts are built as individuals attempt to understand their environment. As learners perceive, compare, and contrast experiences, they arrive at generalizations which enable them to categorize experiences into groups according to common attributes. They must also differentiate these ideas from others. Concurrently, individuals form new categories and expand old ones as they encounter new experiences (Lamberg & Lamb, 1980). Students learn to make generalizations when they are encouraged to analyze their own experiences and form concepts that they can use in meaningful ways, Conceptualization begins with perception, which is the interpretation of the sensory messages that the brain receives. When the brain interprets the sensory stimuli, perception takes place. This is the first step toward forming concepts. Much more is needed, however, for the individual to build a concept. He or she must categorize the concept by distinguishing it from other concepts. This the learner does by noting how an object or idea relates to other objects or ideas in terms of common attributes. Students develop concepts by first perceiving the basic elements of an idea or object; for example, the basic perceptions about a boat would include its color, size, and that it sails on water. Later, some abstract ideas are learned, such as: "It is a means of transportation," "It may be used commercially or for pleasure." As students accumulate these and other perceptual experiences, they develop the ability to form concepts and to generalize.

Students must also be taught to make generalizations. The ability to make generalizations enables them to respond to experiences by classifying stimuli that appear to be alike into the same or different categories according to *critical* or *variable* characteristics. The most concrete way of teaching students to categorize concepts is through practical experiences involving associational activities which help them to identify similarities and differences between and among various concepts. Teachers and trainers should avoid teaching concepts out of context. When students examine concepts in context, they can utilize their language facility and prior knowledge to help them to grasp the concepts. It must be remembered, however, that context is only useful when students can relate background experiences to the new concept to be learned.

Before meaningful learning can take place, students need to develop the ability to build concepts. Concept attainment, however, is a very complex task which demands several complex skills. It takes time for students to develop the ability to conceptualize. As much as is possible, teachers and trainers should provide students with hands-on experiences that will help them establish, clarify, and use the concepts they have learned. The experiences provided should be within the range of the students' understanding. Abstract concepts are difficult to teach and are best taught by relating abstractions to as many concrete experiences as possible.

Educators must also understand that it is important to consider the student's level of cognitive development in presenting a concept or particular aspect of that concept. For example, a student may be ready to deal with the object concept of "table" but may not be ready to deal with the aspect of "table the matter" or "laying a matter on the table." Teachers and trainers should ensure that the concepts students form are correct, clear, and within the learners' range of understanding. Misconceptions are not only difficult to correct, they affect the learning of new concepts. The basis for concept development in young children, as well as students with learning problems, is the provision of first-hand experiences involving the visual, tactile, auditory, and kinesthetic senses. All students can and must develop the ability to form concepts. Some students' innate capacity may limit how much and/or how fast they learn, or what level of complexity of a concept they may be able to handle, but this does not mean that they will not be able to develop adequate understanding of concepts.

Students will never completely develop the ability to conceptualize unless teachers and trainers provide them with real-life opportunities to learn and apply concepts.

THE FUNCTIONAL APPROACH
TO CONCEPT DEVELOPMENT

Utilizing a functional approach to build concepts requires teachers and trainers, first of all, to assess, on an individual basis, the level and relevance of a student's prior knowledge and background experiences. This assessment may consist, in part, of data collected through interviews with parents and other caregivers. During these conferences, teachers and trainers should ask pertinent questions designed to elicit the student's previous experiences in the home and community and his or her interests and preferences. For example, "What chores has your child done in the home?" "Where has the child been in the community, and where does he or she ask to be taken?" "With what toys does he or she play, and what toys does the youngster ask for?" "What jingles, songs, and nursery rhymes does he or she enjoy, sing, and hum along with?" "What foods and beverages does your child enjoy and ask for?" "What stories does he or she like to be told?" "What stories does your youngster like read to him or her?" "What games does your child like to play?" As a further part of the teacher–parent conference, it might be instructive to give the parent or caregiver several objects, photographs, or pictures of these objects and ask him or her to show how the parent or caregiver would teach the child the name of and something about the object. This sample of a parent or caregiver–child interaction might provide insight into the quality as well as the nature of the child's background experiences as provided by the child's "first" teacher(s).

For example, it would be valuable to observe whether the parent or caregiver simply named the object and asked the child to repeat its name, or if the parent or caregiver spoke of any of the object's attributes. If the parent or caregiver does communicate attributes of the object, are they variable attributes that might be used to define other related objects or are they critical variables that differentiate it from other objects? As a case in point, when showing pictures of a cow and a bull to the child, did the parent or caregiver discuss both variable and critical attributes? "This is a picture of a cow. A cow is a farm animal. Look at this sack underneath the cow's belly. It is the cow's udder. It contains milk, and when someone or a machine squeezes these udders, we get milk. We also get leather from a cow.

Now let's look at the picture of the other farm animal. It looks a lot like a cow, but look it doesn't have any udders. It isn't a cow; it is a bull. Like the cow, we get leather from its skin, and some people eat the meat that comes from a bull."

Teachers and trainers may wish to supplement information on prior knowledge and background experiences by designing and implementing exploratory lessons in which assessment data are sought. For example, they may show the student a series of photographs and pictures of fruits and vegetables to determine which ones the student can name and describe. For those foods that were unknown to the student, teachers then should name each and explore its characteristics. This should then be followed up with the functional application of this new information with a variety of direct and indirect experiences. For example, engage the student in supermarket role plays in which he or she is expected to buy certain fruits for a fruit salad and specific vegetables for soup in preparation for a class luncheon honoring "Grandparents Day."

Once teachers and trainers have some insight into the student's prior knowledge and past experiences, they must next determine which objects from among the universe of existing objects have functional value to the individual student. The functional value of an object to a particular student must also be assessed on an individual basis, that is:

1. What concepts should the student possess in order to function as independently and successfully as possible at his or her current level of functioning? Is the student capable of learning and does he or she need, for example, to be able to name only the major body parts when trying to communicate pain or discomfort, or can the child be taught to be more exact in specifying location. "My wrist, elbow, shoulder, ankle, or knee hurts!"

2. What concepts does the student need to develop in order to meet the expectations of caregivers as well as teachers and trainers? Is the student capable of learning and would the child function better at home if the student understood the concept of how to button his or her sweater? It will then be necessary for both teachers and caregivers to show the student various articles of clothing with functioning (not merely decorative) buttons and to explain that buttons found on clothing are usually small, round objects that help people keep their clothing closed for privacy, warmth, and good grooming. When they are found on one particular item of clothing, buttons are usually all the same color, shape, size,

and design and have corresponding button holes through which they are fastened.

In essence, teachers and trainers must assist students in developing a basic oral-receptive and oral-expressive vocabulary needed by the youngsters to function on a daily basis in various functional settings and situations. For the young student, a functional vocabulary might include the names and concepts for:

1. Parts of the face and body;
2. Bodily functions;
3. Foods and beverages;
4. Eating utensils (glasses, cups, saucers, plates, etc.);
5. Cooking utensils and equipment (pots and pans);
6. Household appliances;
7. Rooms of the house;
8. Household materials and equipment;
9. Household tasks;
10. Articles of clothing;
11. Washing and grooming materials and equipment;
12. Household cleaning equipment and supplies;
13. Furniture and furnishings;
14. Vehicles (baby carriages, wagons, tricycles, bicycles, cars, trucks, buses, trains, and airplanes);
15. Pets and plants;
16. Weather conditions (snow, rain, cloudy, and sunny);
17. First aid materials;
18. Relationship names (father, mother, uncle, aunt, cousin, etc.);
19. Stores and shops;
20. Toys and games, including play areas (parks, playgrounds, and schoolyards);
21. Service people (police officers, fire fighters, mail carriers, doctors, dentists, etc.);
22. Recreation sites (movies, skating rinks, bowling alleys, etc.).

For the older student, in addition to the above, a functional vocabulary might include the names and concepts for:

1. Sports and sporting events;
2. Careers and occupations;
3. Hobbies and arts and crafts;
4. Community agencies and centers (library, hospital, recreation center, post office, civic center, etc.);
5. Community businesses and industries;
6. Restaurants and prepared foods;
7. Dating and sex-related terms;
8. Community activities;

9. Legal matters plus civic duties and responsibilities;
10. Travel and transportation;
11. Household service personnel (plumbers, electricians, carpenters, etc.);
12. Financial transactions.

The development of an understanding of concepts involving ideas is clearly more difficult; as, unlike objects, they cannot be seen, heard, touched, or manipulated. Ideas, however, also need to be developed from a functional perspective. The idea of *reciprocity,* for example, is a key functional idea. It is an essential element in maintaining friendships and in fostering satisfactory relationships with classmates, co-workers, neighbors, acquaintances, and relatives. Teachers and trainers must provide learning experiences that build this concept. This might involve explaining how they have *reciprocated* in the past. "My friend, Leon, invited me to dinner twice this past month; it is my *turn* to invite him or take him out to dinner." "Many of the members of my church sent me plants, flowers, fruit baskets, balloons, and 'Get Well' cards when I was in the hospital. Howard, a member of my Bible-study group is in the hospital now. I'll *reciprocate* by sending him a plant and a 'Get Well' card." "Aunt Eleanor has called me long-distance several times this month. I guess it's *my turn* to call her." "Each of my co-workers brought refreshments for our morning 'coffee break' this week. If I want to continue to be a part of this group, I'd better take *my turn* tomorrow."

Once the student has been given several illustrations such as these, teachers and trainers should proceed by asking the student to identify what he or she would consider special favors or friendly deeds that should be *reciprocated,* that is, they deserve a favor or friendly deed in *return.* For each example offered by the student, teachers and trainers should assist the student in identifying the possible ways to *reciprocate.* They should then check to make certain that the student can verbalize his or her understanding of the concept by giving instances in the student's life when a family member, friend, neighbor, or classmate *reciprocated* for the youth's friendly behaviors and when he or she *reciprocated* for the favors of others.

Some additional ideas having functional value that teachers and trainers should develop include:

1. Sharing;
2. Cooperation;
3. Rights, privileges, responsibilities, requirements, and duties;
4. Good behavior, manners, and etiquette (also their opposites: misbehavior, rudeness, vulgarity, etc.);
5. Morals and values;
6. Communication;

7. Self-respect, respect for others, self-discipline, and self-control;
8. Cleanliness;
9. Privacy;
10. Fashion, style, convention, and conformity;
11. Assistance and advice;
12. Careers and occupations;
13. Salary, wages, minimum wage, employee, employer, and fringe benefits;
14. Hospitalization and insurance (medical, household, life, disability, group, etc.);
15. Social security;
16. Net and gross pay, deductions, taxes, and contributions;
17. Deposits, withdrawals, interest, and penalties;
18. Mortgages, rent, leases, down payments, escrow, and bids;
19. Elections, voting, candidates, political parties, democrats, and republicans;
20. Ecology, pollution, recycling, beautifying, and conservation;
21. Loyalty;
22. Liberty, freedom, and democracy;
23. Diversity, race, nationality, religion, ethnicity, and disability.

These are merely some of the functional ideas that, depending on the student's level of functioning and background experiences, should be addressed by teachers and trainers in the building of concepts.

Sample Instructional Plan 1

Topic Area: Building Concepts

Designed by: Thor Stratton

Time Recommended: 45 Minutes

Background Information

The student infrequently interacts with her peers. During playground, physical education classes, and free time, she generally plays by herself.

(continued)

Sample Instructional Plan 1 *(cont.)*

Annual Goal (or General Objective)

The student will initiate, organize, and participate in team sports activities with classmates during playground, physical education classes, and recess.

Short-Term Instructional Objective

The student will develop the concepts for objects used in leisure time activities.

Cognitive Dimensions

1. Differentiating between and among various objects used in team and other sports activities;
2. Comprehending the rules of various games and sports;
3. Locating and obtaining needed equipment and materials;
4. Selecting an appropriate setting for the game to take place;
5. Setting aside an appropriate amount of time to play the game;
6. Selecting the correct number of players for the game;
7. Observing the rules of the game during play;
8. Scoring the game.

Functional Context

The student will develop the skills involved in acquiring and maintaining friendships.

Lesson Objective

When the student is shown a basketball, a football, a handball, a tennis ball, and a medicine ball, and asked to:

1. Point to the basketball,
2. Point to the ones that are not basketballs,
3. Say the name of the basketball,

she will do so correctly on three separate occasions.

Materials and Equipment

1. Cardboard carton;
2. Basketball, football, handball, medicine ball, and tennis ball;

(continued)

Sample Instructional Plan 1 *(cont.)*

3. Wastebasket;
4. Video cassette of a basketball game;
5. Video player and television monitor.

Motivating Activity

Play a game of catch with each of the balls used in the lesson.

Instructional Procedures

1. Show the student the basketball. Encourage her to look at it and explore it with her hands. Tell her to bounce it several times. Tell the student to totally describe the experience. After she has done so, demonstrate your own exploration strategies while saying, "A basketball is round. I can bounce it with one hand, but I must use two hands to catch it because it is so big. I can throw the basketball into the air and I must catch it with both of my hands because a basketball is so big." Then ask the student to go through the same actions while you say, "You are bouncing the basketball. You bounced the basketball and caught it with your two hands. You threw the basketball in the air and caught it."
2. Then remove each of the other balls from the nearby cardboard carton. Compare each to the basketball. For example, "The medicine ball is also round, but it is much larger than the basketball and cannot be bounced." "The football is not round like a basketball, and, because of its shape, it bounces in all different directions." "A tennis ball is round like a basketball, but it is much smaller and can be bounced and caught easily with one hand." "A handball is round like a basketball, but it, too, is smaller than a basketball and can be bounced and caught easily with one hand."
3. Play a modified basketball game, a one-on-one game, using the classroom wastebasket for your basket. Explain that a basketball is named that way because it is used to play a game in which the purpose is to throw it through the basket.

(continued)

Sample Instructional Plan 1 *(cont.)*

4. Place all the balls on a desk area, and ask the student to point to each one in response to your question, "Where is the _____ball?" Then show her each of the balls and ask her to name the basketball when you point to it. Tell her also to say, "That is not a basketball," for each of the other balls shown to her.
5. Show the student a video of a 5-minute segment of a basketball game. Ask the student to talk about what happened on the screen. During her description, ask questions that will stimulate comments on the actions. Comment on the times the baskets were made, "The basketball went through the basket. A score." Comment also on the times that the baskets were missed. "The basketball didn't go through the basket. No score this time."
6. Ask the student to describe a basketball to you and tell how it is the same and different from other objects used to play games.

Assessment Strategy

Observe the student to see if she identified the basketball correctly on three separate occasions. Record her performance on the Diagnostic Checklist.

Follow-Up Activity or Objective

If the student achieves the lesson objective, proceed to assisting her in initiating, organizing, and participating in several one-on-one basketball games, each time with a different peer.

Sample Instructional Plan 2

Topic Area: Building Concepts
Designed by: Gertrude Frohman
Time Recommended: 1 Hour

(continued)

Sample Instructional Plan 2 *(cont.)*

Background Information

The student is now able to read at the fifth grade level. As part of his transitional program, in preparation for his postschool years, we are working intensively with vocational and leisure time knowledge and skills to increase the likelihood of his successful adaptation to living and working in the community.

Annual Goal (or General Objective)

The student will describe and discuss various leisure time activities that may be available to him.

Short-Term Instructional Objective

The student will develop the skills necessary to plan and engage in leisure time activities involving the use of public transportation.

Cognitive Dimensions

1. Conceptualizing the word, vacation;
2. Interpreting bus, train, and airline schedules;
3. Identifying his personal interests and preferences and correlating them with specific leisure time activities;
4. Identifying the time requirements for traveling to a leisure site and correlating it with the time available to him for that activity;
5. Reading and interpreting advertisements, including travel brochures, that describe available leisure time activities;
6. Selecting leisure time activities, including vacations, that meet his recreational needs as well as time and budgetary constraints.

Functional Context

The student will develop the knowledge and skills necessary to plan and engage in leisure time activities involving public transportation.

(continued)

Sample Instructional Plan 2 *(cont.)*

Lesson Objective

When the student is shown several travel brochures, he will select the brochure that best meets his interests and preferences, as well as time and budgetary constraints. He will describe what a vaction is and what his preferences are for his "ideal" vacation.

Materials and Equipment

1. Teacher-made travel brochures;
2. Commercial travel brochures;
3. Advertisements from newspapers and magazines advertising vacation trips;
4. Video cassette of several commercials for vacation trips;
5. Video player and television monitor.

Motivating Activity

Show the student a video of several commercials advertising vacation trips. Engage him in a discussion of which trips described in the commercials might be of interest to him. If he selects one or more, ask him to describe why he picked it (them). If he selects none of them, ask him to explain why he did not choose any and to describe the kind of place he would like to visit on a trip.

Instructional Procedures

1. Ask the student if he has ever gone on a trip or vacation. If so, ask him to tell you all about it. During the discussion, ask questions that will encourage the student to retrieve prior experiences. After the student has described his experiences, tell him about some vacation trips that you have taken. In your description, be sure to make clear that your vacation was taken at a time when you were not working or going to school and at a place that was away from the usual places you stay or go to (your home and the homes of friends, relatives, and neighbors, the doctor's office, the bowling alley, the movie theater, the supermarket, the library, the department store, etc). Tell about your vacation when you stayed in a motel, hotel, resort, on a boat, at a guest house, or bed-and-

(continued)

Sample Instructional Plan 2 *(cont.)*

breakfast place. Throughout, question him about what one does on a vacation—that is, is it a time for work or a time for recreation to ascertain whether he understands the concept of a vacation as a time of change and rest. If necessary, explain that a vacation is a time to relax, enjoy, and to have new experiences and that it involves travel and staying and sleeping away from home.

2. Proceed to discuss with him your trips into the community and other travel that are *not* vacations. For example: a trip taken out-of-town to visit a sick relative (not a trip for enjoyment or to relax), a trip to a conference you attended to learn new things about teaching, and a trip to the dentist that was not necessarily an enjoyable experience.

3. Then ask him to tell about any vacations that he may have taken with his family. Ask him if he is on vacation today. Tell him to explain to you why or why not. Provide assistance as needed.

4. Discuss with him your preferences for a vacation in terms of climate, topography, and activities. (For example, explain that when the weather is warm, you enjoy mountain scenery and mountain lakes for nice walks to explore the flowers and plants that grow in the mountains.) Then show him teacher-made brochures with cover depictions of: a beach resort, a ski resort, a modern city, and a mountain with a lake in the springtime. Ask him to pick the brochure that you should read to find out more about a possible vacation. Reward him for picking the correct brochure *and* for explaining why that brochure might describe a vacation spot that would be of interest to you.

5. Then show the student commercial brochures and advertisements that offer "springtime in the mountain" vacations. Discuss time and budgetary factors in deciding what vacations are possible. Ask him to pick the brochure he is interested in reading and tell you why he picked that vacation spot.

6. Ask the student to tell you what is a vacation, what a vacation involves, and what activities are not vacations.

(continued)

Sample Instructional Plan 2 *(cont.)*

7. Show the student the video of vacation commercials. Ask him to select a vacation trip he would like to take, again describing why he picked the one chosen.

Assessment Strategy

Listen to the student as he describes what a vacation is and what it is not. Record his performance on the Diagnostic Checklist.

Follow-Up Activity or Objective

If the student achieves the lesson objective, proceed to a new learning experience in which he is expected to read and interpret the information contained in newspaper and magazine advertisements that offer vacation trips.

5

COMPREHENSION

The ultimate goal of instruction is to enable students to comprehend what they are taught and to apply what they have learned in their daily lives. Although many concepts of education are controversial, it is universally accepted that comprehension is crucial to learning since learning cannot occur unless students comprehend.

This chapter examines the comprehension process and describes factors that are important to its development. What is comprehension? How do schemata affect comprehension? What is the role of metacognition in comprehension? What role does questioning play in developing comprehension? These questions are answered in this chapter.

WHAT IS COMPREHENSION?

Interest in understanding what is involved in comprehension is not new. For many years, educators and cognitive psychologists (Huey, 1968; Smith, 1975) have noted the importance of comprehension to reading and learning and have been interested in understanding what occurs when someone comprehends written or oral discourse. While interest in understanding the comprehension process has intensified over the years, the comprehension process itself has not changed. People comprehend today just as they did hundreds of years ago. As Roser (1984) suggests, "Whatever children and adults did as they read in ancient Egypt, Greece, or Rome, and whatever they do today in order to derive or apply meaning to print is the same" (p. 48). As a result of research done in education, psychology, and linguistics, educators now have a better understanding of the comprehension process and how to facilitate it. This improvement in understanding the nature of comprehension should enable instructors to plan more effective strategies to help students develop the ability to comprehend.

In attempting to define comprehension, perhaps it is best to begin by stating what it is not. Comprehension is not only the ability to recognize words and pronounce them meaningfully, even though this is a necessary step in the comprehension process. As was noted in the previous chapter, words are merely labels for ideas. They have no meaning to the individual unless he or she understands the concepts these words represent. Many teachers and trainers have discovered that students do not automatically get meaning from the words that they are able to decode. Comprehension is also not the ability to memorize facts. Many classroom teachers can attest that many students have been able to memorize and reproduce facts that they do not understand and, therefore, are unable to use the information to solve problems or to make applications to their lives. What then is comprehension?

Comprehension is currently viewed as a process by which the individual derives meaning by interacting with the text (Anderson & Pearson, 1984). What the individual understands from reading the text or from listening to oral presentations is derived not merely from the author's words, sentences, or ideas but from the experiences the student has accumulated over the years. As the individual interacts with the author's or speaker's ideas, the learner relates the information to prior knowledge in order to derive meaning. Rubin (1992) affirms, "Comprehension is the process of constructing meaning by taking relevant ideas from the text and relating them to ideas you already have; this is the process of the reader interacting with the text" (p. 5). (The same thing applies in dealing with oral information.) This interaction between the individual and text, written or oral, is the foundation of the comprehension process.

Comprehension is a complex process which defies simple definitions or explanations. It is not a product or a simple observable process which can be directly measured. It is a covert process. What educators observe during instruction is not comprehension but the products of comprehension, such as answers to questions or demonstrations indicating understanding. Students may explain what they learn from reading a selection or from listening to directions, instructions, or explanations. They may verbalize the reasons for their answers or for the steps they take in performing an activity, but the mental processes that actually occur are unobservable. In discussing the complex nature of comprehension, Rubin (1992) notes that the ability to comprehend written information depends on the ability to comprehend spoken language. Familiarity with the arrangement of words and the ability to discriminate among words in oral language enhances the ability to comprehend written language. Research (Jolly,

1980; Young, 1936) indicates that there is a significant correlation between listening comprehension and reading comprehension. Students who did poorly in listening comprehension also did poorly in reading comprehension.

Although it is not possible to state definitively how comprehension occurs or how one processes oral or written information, it appears that good comprehenders have certain characteristics. For example, they decode quickly, have large vocabularies and phonemic awareness, know about text features, and use several strategies to aid comprehension and meaning (Paris, Wasik, & Turner, 1991).

Comprehension is a multifaceted process which involves many skills. It involves the individual's schemata, language facility (ability to decode words and understanding of syntax and semantics of the language), and the ability to conceptualize. Roe et al. (1991) have compiled several generalizations to explain the process. The following is one of them. In their view, comprehension is a thinking process during which the individual strives to obtain meaning and to monitor his or her learning.

Comprehension involves getting the author's or speaker's explicit as well as implicit meaning. Often both meanings are derived simultaneously (Lamberg & Lamb, 1980). Comprehension also includes the ability to evaluate, make judgments, and develop new ideas based on the information presented. Tonjes & Zintz (1981) divide comprehension into four levels: literal, interpretive or inferential, critical, and creative. Each level is cumulative and is interrelated with the other levels. Each level is also interdependent on the other levels in that each builds on the other levels.

1. *Literal Level.* This level requires that the individual grasps main ideas and supporting details which were explicitly stated. He or she must also understand sequencing and must be able to translate what the person has read or heard in his or her own words.

    Because much of what an author or speaker desires to communicate is not explicitly stated but is implied, if students do not go beyond this literal level, comprehension of the information presented would be incomplete. Nothing is wrong with solely comprehending at the literal level. This level forms the basis for understanding at the other levels. One must first understand the basic facts before one can understand those that are implied or before one is able to use the information in meaningful ways. In order to comprehend at higher levels, therefore, one must first understand and remember the facts as presented. Comprehension involves thinking. There are various levels of thinking—so there are various levels of comprehension. Higher level comprehension requires the ability to think and comprehend at the lower levels. It is the reliance on the literal level, however, to the exclusion of other levels, that elicits criticism of this level.

2. *Interpretive, or Inferential, Level.* Comprehension at this level involves making inferences, drawing conclusions, making judgments and generalizations, summarizing, and comparing and contrasting. To gain understanding at this level, the learner must be able to interpret figurative language, solve problems, and deal with abstract ideas. Obviously, slow learners or those with learning disabilities will experience difficulty working at this level. The learner must use information gained at the literal level, combined with background experiences to arrive at those meanings that are implicitly stated. It is at this level that many students begin to experience difficulty in comprehending. The learner must go beyond this level, however, to derive further meaning and to understand more fully the author's or speaker's message.

3. *Critical Level.* At this level, the individual evaluates information by making judgments. He or she evaluates the author's or speaker's purpose, mood, and authenticity. The individual also evaluates the material in terms of his or her purpose(s) for processing the information. To derive meaning at this level, the learner seeks answers to questions such as: "What is the author's or speaker's purpose?" "Does he or she intend to persuade, instruct, or entertain me?" "Is the information fact or opinion?" "Can it be verified?" "Is it appropriate?" Having discovered the author's or speaker's purpose(s), in light of the facts presented and prior knowledge, the student then adjusts learning strategies to match his or her purpose(s) for listening or reading. Critical comprehension involves the ability to reason logically and to make judgments. Good comprehenders are good logical thinkers who have the ability to make sound judgments based on careful evaluation of information.

4. *Creative Level.* This is the level at which the learner uses the author's or speaker's message to form new and related ideas or items or develop new solutions. This level involves producing novel ideas to solve problems and new ways of viewing incidents, people, and things. Creative learners consider information from perspectives other than the one presented and are able to look beyond the obvious and produce new or alternate ways of solving problems. These individuals use

divergent thinking skills to go beyond the literal, interpretive, and critical comprehension levels and create new ideas.

Instructors should realize that students operating at this level must not be forced to think convergently. Rather than looking for right and wrong answers to questions or right and wrong ways of demonstrating understanding, teachers and trainers need to examine the line of reasoning the individual uses, the type of assumptions he or she makes based on the facts, and the purpose for processing the information.

Creative thinking does not occur hurriedly or on command. It develops spontaneously and takes time. Wallas (1926) suggested that there are four stages of the creative process for most people: (1) *Preparation*—this involves all the necessary background experiences, skills, and prior knowledge in a particular field; (2) *Incubation*—this involves the time during which the individual mulls over or thinks through an idea; (3) *Illumination*—this is the moment when insight dawns and solutions appear; and (4) *Verification*—this involves the final stage when the individual tests his or her hypotheses or refines his or her findings.

If students are expected to operate at this level, instructors must not only create an atmosphere conducive to creativity, they must also give students time to think and the freedom to think divergently and not merely produce the pat answers teachers might expect.

Although it is convenient to discuss the four levels of comprehension separately, it does not follow that these levels are separate, unrelated parts of a process. Teachers and trainers should not attempt to teach these levels in a disjointed, separate, unintegrated manner. Comprehension is a process involving four unified, integrated levels. The processing of information at one level does not have to be completed in order for another level to begin or end. All of the levels are interrelated and interdependent.

FACTORS INFLUENCING COMPREHENSION

The most important factors that influence comprehension are schemata, language facility, affective development, and metacognition. Each of these factors is discussed separately for emphasis and clarity. It must not be construed, however, that the components operate independently of one another. Like the levels of comprehension, they are interrelated and interdependent.

Schemata

The schema theory is providing new insights on comprehension. Schema (singular), or schemata (plural), as described in the previous chapter, represents the concepts that the individual has developed through experiences. One of the most important conclusions drawn from recent research (Adams & Bertram, 1980; Durkin, 1981; Pearson, 1979) is the vital role of students' schemata in facilitating comprehension at all levels, but particularly at the levels beyond the literal. Students must use prior knowledge and ideas in conjunction with new information to create meaning. Background experiences and schemata are sometimes viewed synonymously. However, there is an important difference between the two. An individual has many and varied experiences each day. Some of these experiences are meaningful in terms of how they affect one's knowledge, life, or goals, and some are not. Some are understood, and others are not. Many of these experiences could be viewed as a large box of unsorted and unfiled materials. Schemata, on the other hand, represent a meaningful filing system of all background experiences and prior knowledge. Schemata are cognitive structures or frameworks into which all types of experiences and knowledge are filed. In schemata, experiences on a given topic are grouped meaningfully (Pearson & Johnson, 1977). For example, anyone who travels by train frequently has schemata of trains and procedures involved in traveling by rail. These schemata also include train stations—train schedules, the ticket counter, conductors, baggage check-in, baggage claim, and boarding gate. When an individual who travels by train enters the train station, he or she uses schemata to identify various locations at the station and to execute the traveling procedure. Each traveler's schemata supply structures for integrating all types of new information (Roe et al., 1991).

McNeil (1992) succinctly describes schemata this way: "Schemata are the reader's [listener's] concepts, beliefs, expectations, processes—virtually everything from past experiences that are used in making sense of things and actions. . . . Schemata are used to make sense of texts; the printed word evokes the reader's experiences, as well as past and potential relationships" (p. 19). Roe et al. (1991) believe schemata are: "Related clusters of concepts based on knowledge and experience [and] are related to word knowledge and to the comprehension process" (p. 25). According to the schema theory, (a single cluster of experiences or knowledge) oral or written information is meaningless unless the reader or listener "reads" meaning into it. Those students who comprehend well have the ability to relate what they already know to the new information to be learned.

Teachers and trainers of all subjects must be aware of three types of schemata. One is the *domain,* which involves knowledge of specific topics, ideas, textural format, or processes for understanding a particular subject. Instructors of various subject areas must assist students in developing background knowledge required for comprehending materials in a given area. Another type of schema is *general knowledge* needed to understand social conventions that are common to several situations. This general knowledge enables an individual to draw appropriate inferences and relate to other people and events in meaningful ways. A third type of schema has to do with accepted *conventions of language.* This includes understanding the structure, syntax, and usage of the particular language community to which the individual belongs. The individual must understand and be able to use language in order to communicate effectively with others (McNeil, 1992).

Individuals use schemata to draw inferences, to make predictions, to form hypotheses, and to anticipate writer's or speaker's ideas. The ability to anticipate ideas in written or oral discourse increases comprehension (Adams & Collins, 1986). Students who do not have the experiences related to the actual subject or topic they are expected to comprehend, lack the schemata necessary to anticipate meaning or to understand written or oral materials on these topics. Every area of the student's life is affected by his or her schemata. For instance, an individual is able to understand a sporting event or the sport's section of a newspaper better if the person has schemata for sports. The more extensive and relevant an individual's schemata are to a specific topic, the better he or she will comprehend that topic. If the individual has limited or no experience with a particular topic, the person will have insufficient or no schemata to activate, and comprehension of that topic will be difficult or impossible. If the individual has no frame of reference from which to process new information, comprehension will be limited. Schemata, therefore, form the foundation for comprehending new ideas. They are structures of knowledge, ideas, information, and concepts that are constructed in the individual's mind through experiences. Teachers and trainers must plan experiences that will build schemata to assist students to comprehend written as well as oral information. They also need to help students to select the appropriate schemata to apply to the new information. When students experience difficulty in using their background experiences for comprehension, instructors need to ascertain whether the learners lack the necessary information or are unable to utilize existing schemata in order to cocmprehend (Jones, 1982). If students lack the schemata, teachers should plan direct and vicarious experiences to help them. During comprehension, the reader or listener combines ideas from the "text" with information in his or her schemata. If the individual does not have the schemata for a particular subject or concept and sufficient information is then provided, the student may form a new schema for that topic (Cooper, 1986).

For students to make maximum use of their prior knowledge in attempting to comprehend new information, teachers and trainers must teach the students how to activate schemata—that is, find out what information they already have on a particular topic that they have to learn. Teachers may take several steps to help students learn to assess their prior knowledge. First, they must be taught the importance of schemata in comprehending new material. Second, they must be taught how to activate schemata by asking questions such as: "What do I already know that will help me comprehend this topic or idea?" "Is this information relevant?" Third, instructors may model the steps they take in assessing their own prior knowledge by asking themselves questions, answering them, and then demonstrating how they combine prior knowledge and new information in order to comprehend.

Language

An individual's language facility plays a significant role in comprehension. Knowledge of his or her language and the ability to use it efficiently is crucial to comprehension. The learner must be able to discriminate visually and orally between and among sounds and words. The learner must also understand the syntax—that is, the relationship of words to one another. The learner must also understand the semantics of the language—that is, the denotative as well as connotative meanings.

The student's oral language ability is an important factor that teachers and trainers must consider when teaching comprehension. Research has indicated that a significant correlation exists between a student's oral language ability and comprehension (Loban, 1963; Menyuk, 1984). A student's oral language facility is directly related to the development of his or her schemata and, consequently, to learning in general. Loban's (1976) longitudinal study of the language development of more than 200 children from the age of 5 to 18 years revealed the importance of oral language proficiency in learning. The children in the study who were proficient in oral language in kindergarten and the first grade, before they were able to read and write, were the same children who excelled in reading and writing when they reached the sixth grade and above. Students with limited oral language ability or whose primary language is not English will lack the knowledge and skills necessary to understand the basic forms of English and the concepts represented by this particular language.

These students will, therefore, experience difficulty in comprehension. Oral language ability is important at every stage of the student's learning, not just at the primary level. Language acquisition is developmental, and no one is able to learn all the lexicon or meanings of his or her indigenous language; however, a certain level of language competence is necessary to comprehend at each level of learning.

Cognitive Development

As discussed in Chapter 1, cognitive development influences all areas of learning. The learner's level of cognitive development will determine what he or she is able to comprehend. A student at the sensorimotor level, for example, will lack the mental development and schemata to understand ideas that those individuals operating at the formal operational level are able to comprehend. Teachers and trainers must be aware of the student's level of cognitive development and plan activities at the level at which the student can function most effectively.

Affective Development

The individual's interests, self-concepts, beliefs, attitudes, feelings, and motivation may have profound impact on how much or if he or she comprehends. The way the learner feels about him- or herself, the instructor, and the subject often influence what the learner is able to achieve. A student may possess the skills needed to comprehend, but his or her attitude may interfere with his or her ability to apply those skills in order to comprehend. Interests and motivation may determine the effort one puts forth to achieve comprehension. Similarly, if the learner believes that the new information or idea is unnecessary, unimportant, is antipathal to his or her morals or an affront to his or her dignity, the student may create mental or emotional blocks which may counteract or limit comprehension.

To maximize the chances that students will comprehend what they are taught, teachers and trainers must be aware of these factors affecting comprehension. They must know the linguistic and cognitive level at which each student is functioning and also determine what prior knowledge the student has or will need to learn new material. The teacher or trainer must provide direct or indirect experiences, if the learner does not have the relevant schemata, interest, or motivation. It is very important that teachers and trainers utilize student schemata as bridges to assist them in going from the known to the unknown as they present new materials for students to learn. Much time is lost in reteaching and remediation because instructors fail to assess prior knowledge and experiences before teaching new information.

There are several ways of assessing a student's prior knowledge. One of the primary means of analyzing a learner's schemata is by asking the learner questions. Questions can be used to gather information on travel experiences, hobbies, interests, and recreational activities. Observations can also yield valuable insights on background experiences and prior knowledge. Other methods of assessing what students already know about a particular topic as well as other relevant background experiences which will impact favorably on the learning situation are: classroom discussions, informal conversations with students, listening to students as they communicate with one another, and by having one-on-one conferences with students. These are, perhaps, the best ways of assessing a student's schemata.

No amount of effort will make every student comprehend a particular topic or subject at the same speed or level as other students. Nevertheless, it is necessary to know how much preparation is needed to teach a student at the basic level of competence and also to understand which student requires such preparation.

Metacognition and Comprehension

Some educators dismiss the term metacognition as a fad; however, research on metacognition and the role it plays in comprehension is providing new insights into how to teach comprehension (Bloom, 1956; Heller, 1986; Palincsar & Brown, 1984; Paris & Myers, 1981). Metacognition is the method of monitoring one's thought and activities as one processes information. Metacognition enables the readers to become aware of what they know and what they do not know (McNeil, 1992). It is the learner's awareness of his or her cognitive functions. There are two components of metacognition: (1) Understanding of the skills and resources necessary to do a task and (2) Knowing when one has achieved success or what course to take to overcome blocks or interferences to comprehension (Baker & Brown, 1984). Both aspects of metacognition play an important role in comprehension. Research indicates that learners who comprehend well monitor their comprehension and are able to use corrective strategies to ensure comprehension (Baker & Brown, 1984). As students monitor their own thoughts and understanding, they can try different strategies if they discover that their comprehension has broken down. Competent listeners and readers are aware of what they need to know and the different purposes of processing information and are able to adjust their knowledge to achieve success. Metacognitive abilities help the learner to understand how well he or she is comprehending. Learners are constantly asking themselves questions as they process information. They ask such questions as: "Am I understanding?"

"What is it that I need to know?" "Do I have any prior knowledge on this topic?" "What are the key ideas?" Self-questioning facilitates comprehension because it also helps students keep their minds on the task, thus avoiding distractions. It also helps students clarify ideas and purpose as they test how much and what they are learning.

CRITERIA FOR GUIDING COMPREHENSION DEVELOPMENT

Students do not develop the ability to comprehend automatically. They must receive systematic, well-planned instruction. Meaningful learning from texts or oral communication depends on the student's ability to comprehend the information presented. It is extremely important that teachers and trainers understand this and plan every lesson with comprehension as the primary goal. Every lesson should be planned to meet this important objective, because if students do not comprehend what is taught, valuable time is wasted and future learning may be adversely affected. Cooper (1986) suggests five principles for guiding comprehension development. They are:

1. As was mentioned earlier, one of the major factors in developing the ability to comprehend is the individual's schemata. Research on schemata clearly supports the principle that background experiences influence comprehension. Instructional programs aimed at building comprehension must therefore incorporate strategies that will assist students in activating or developing background experiences, concepts, and ideas relative to a specific topic and relate that schemata to new information to be learned. Teachers and trainers should model how they recall prior experiences and relate schemata to new information.

2. Comprehension is a covert process during which the individual constructs meaning while interacting with the texts. To help students get meaning from written information, instructors must help them to understand text formats, emphasizing such aspects as sentence structure, types of paragraphs, paragraph structure, and meaning clues. Instructors must also help students see how understanding these features aids in processing information and ultimately in comprehending.

3. The comprehension process consists of several skills and levels which should not be construed as ends in themselves or as separate skills of the total process. Comprehension skills should be taught with reference to the student's schemata and the new information, not as isolated skills. Students must be

taught to use the skills as clues or as means to achieve their primary goal, comprehension.

4. The manner in which each student comprehends is directly related to his or her prior experiences. Teachers and trainers should, therefore, take individual differences into account as they instruct students and as they evaluate the student's responses. Instructors should be prepared to accept divergent responses as long as those responses are logical and can be substantiated. Critical and creative comprehension will be stifled if instructors expect similar responses from all students.

5. Comprehension is a linguistic process and should be taught as part of the whole language arts program that includes: listening, speaking, reading, and writing. The student's oral language facility forms the base for comprehension of the written language. Therefore, instructional strategies in reading comprehension should build on and extend the student's oral language. Teachers should seek every opportunity to provide students with activities through which they can develop and utilize their listening, speaking, reading, and writing experiences.

These five principles do not represent an exhaustive list for developing comprehension. These should, however, provide teachers and trainers with a base from which to develop effective comprehension programs which will guide students in developing their comprehension ability.

ROLE OF QUESTIONS IN DEVELOPING COMPREHENSION

The types of questions teachers ask definitely affect the level of comprehension that the students achieve or whether they comprehend at all. Many classroom questions do not encourage students to think, draw on prior knowledge, or find solutions. Such queries merely evoke rote answers. Napell (1978) classified other types of ineffective questions that are not likely to encourage students to develop their comprehension ability. They are:

1. Dead-end questions that require yes-no answers. These questions are often addressed to a whole group of students to satisfy the instructor's conscience that he or she has gotten the ideas across to the students. For example, "Do you all understand the main idea?" This question implies, "I hope all of you have gotten the main idea because I am ready to move on."

2. The run-on question which includes several unrelated questions asked at the same time. For example, "What did the man see?" "Are you going to read the other book?" "Did you bring a pencil to school?" Students are not given the opportunity to answer any of these before the next question is asked.

3. The program-question which requires students to give the answer(s) that the teacher wants and no other. These questions inhibit divergent thinking. They do not permit students to think, express their own ideas, or to speculate. For example, "Tell me exactly what Paul did." "Was he really no good?" "Did a really great opportunity present itself?"

4. The put-down question which teachers ask when they do not want students to further query the instructor. Teachers ask these types of questions because they want to discourage students from asking questions that instructors decide are unnecessary. For example, "I have explained this material to you several times and I'm sure you know it by now. Do you have any more questions?" Most students would be unwilling to embarrass themselves in the presence of other students by admitting that they were unable to comprehend after "so many explanations." Since self-concept is closely tied to learning, anything that threatens the self-concept will affect comprehension.

5. The ambiguous question which confuses students by obscuring what answer is really required. These questions also limit assessment of the student's comprehension, because the instructor is unable to determine if the student knows the concept or does not understand the question or vice versa. For example, "If you had 4 apples and you shared them with Jack, exactly how many would you have left?" Here the teacher is expecting the answer "2" because he or she assumes that the student understands "share" to mean divide equally.

Another problem with reference to teachers' questions is that they use questions mainly to discover how much factual information a student has learned and can reproduce (Alexander et al., 1983). The role of questions in instruction, however, is not merely to evaluate, but also to help students to activate schemata, stimulate critical and creative thinking, and to develop a sense of inquiry. Teachers and trainers should prepare thoughtful questions which will elicit answers at the interpretive, critical, and creative levels of comprehension. They should also guide students in asking themselves and others questions.

Teachers and trainers should also help students to develop their own questions which they can use to explore their own curiosities, identify problems, and find solutions. It is very important that teachers do this, because usually most of the questions asked in the learning environment are raised only by the teachers. Students are often neither given time to ask questions nor are they encouraged to ask questions. This is unfortunate because learning to ask themselves, other students, and teachers questions would help learners to activate schemata, understand the teacher's questions, and understand the new information they are expected to learn. Teachers and trainers can help students to comprehend better by taking time to prepare good questions and by giving students sufficient time to think and then answer questions, as well as by teaching and encouraging students to ask themselves questions.

THE FUNCTIONAL APPROACH TO THE DEVELOPMENT OF COMPREHENSION

This section deals with the functional approaches to the development of oral and written comprehension.

Oral Comprehension

The ability to comprehend a speaker's message is vital for effective communication. Teachers and trainers must pay particular attention to the development of oral language comprehension because of its fundamental role in early and continuing interpersonal communication and its quintessential role in the development of cognition.

In order for individuals to interact satisfactorily with others, they must be able to utilize their previous experiences and language facility to arrive at an understanding of the content of the speaker's message. They must also be able to draw inferences, make generalizations, analyze, make applications, and make judgments.

Among the settings in which oral language comprehension develops are the home, school, and the community.

The Home

In the home, students must be able to respond to their own name and to understand and react appropriately to the names for the different persons, places, and things in their environment, so that they may locate persons and/or items when asked to look at, point to, show, or find them. Students must be able to comprehend the words used by adults that indicate actions to be engaged in as adults direct them to touch, pick up, hold, pass, manipulate, play with, and bring the adults various toy and real objects. Students need to participate with increasing understanding in the various types of oral language experiences in the home. They must understand that they should terminate a behavior when admonished "No!," and to continue a behavior when told to do so. During their daily interactions in the home, they may be expected to respond to a variety of questions: "What?" "Where?" "When?" "Whose?" "How?" "How many?" "Did you?" "Have you?" and "Why?" They are asked to carry out various simple and multipart directions and commands. Learners must show a clear understanding of the grammar of the language and the relationship of words to one another.

There are a host of other work-related, play-related, and learning-related functional expectations and requirements as children carry out the various activities of daily living in the home. Children must comprehend the oral language messages and then meaningfully engage in countless essential activities and routines, especially those involving health and safety maintenance: resting and sleeping, and health and safety rules and regulations. "It's bedtime!" "Time for your nap!" "Stay away from the stove!" "Don't forget to take your vitamins!" "Only one cookie for dessert!" Adults may require students to observe routines that are critical to the development of self-care skills such as: toileting, dressing and undressing, eating and drinking, grooming, and household management. In dealing with these actions, they may be asked to respond to such questions and directives as: "Do you have to go to the bathroom?" "Do you need help in taking off your sweater?" "Hold your fork like this otherwise you'll spill your food!" "Turn on the cold water first, then the hot water, regulate the temperature, and then wash your face and hands so that you won't burn yourself!" "Watch me as I show you how to use the dish towel to dry the dishes!" As they grow older, students will be expected to participate in more advanced communication which calls for decision making and problem resolution based on interaction with family and friends.

Learners must be able to interpret idiomatic, figurative, and colloquial speech. They need to react appropriately by stopping a disturbing behavior when mother says, "Boy, I'm beginning to lose my cool!" They might prepare themselves for a late dinner because "Daddy is tied up at the office!" and they are less likely to be confused when told "Don't throw the baby out with the bath water!" Throughout all these family and household communications, they must be able to comprehend literally, interpretatively, critically, and creatively to innumerable oral communications and underlying supportive non-verbal elements.

The School and the Community

In the ideal classroom, students are expected to comprehend directions and instructions, both written and oral, to respond correctly to well-formulated questions, to listen and interpret explanations, to grasp main ideas, to remember details and sequences, to make inferences, draw conclusions, make wise judgments, arrive at logical generalizations, compare and contrast elements, solve problems, deal with abstract ideas, and suggest innovative solutions. The role of learner is indeed a functional life role whether it takes place in school or not.

As students grow older and participate in the world of work, they must understand the specifications and dimensions of their work assignments, the rules and regulations of the workplace, and the nature and intent of interpersonal communications, whether from supervisors or co-workers.

As participants in leisure-time pursuits, people will be instructed by fellow participants or recreational personnel in recreation-specific knowledge, skills, and values. Individuals will need to acquire such fundamental information as the nature of the activity, the costs of participation, time requirements and constraints, requisite materials and equipment, task elements, and the location and availability of specific activities.

As responsible and responsive citizens, students will need to learn about their community so that they may function successfully in that community, reaping its benefits, contributing to its success, and ensuring its continuing existence.

As consumers of goods and services, people need to comprehend the rules of the marketplace, how to make and live within a budget, and how to maximize their buying power. They need to understand information concerning financial transactions and about investments from professionals as well as their nonprofessional relatives and friends.

As travelers in their local community and in the larger world, individuals need to acquire the necessary information so they can travel to work, to leisure-time centers, and to the other places in their lives with judicious attention paid to cost, time, and comfort factors. In many circumstances throughout their lives as functional learners, students must "read" and interpret and then act appropriately based on their understanding of the relevant information with which they are provided. Teachers and trainers must provide students with a variety of learning experiences that prepare them for those life situations when they will need to learn from others by assisting learners in the development of oral language comprehension.

As members of a community and as responsible and responsive participants in the life of the community, individuals must respond appropriately to a variety of oral messages, whether coming from human service professionals such as librarians, physicians, dentists, or therapists or if proffered by other service personnel such as store clerks, police officers, fire fighters, security guards, workers at election sites, train conductors, aerobics instructors, and receptionists. For example, when they are told of their various symptoms and possible treatments by health care providers, individuals must then deal with factors such as dosages, when to take medicine, and being asked to analyze how they have responsed to medicinal and nonpharmacological treatments.

When one is lost in the community one needs to understand, retain, and retrieve directions provided to them. Individuals must be able to interpret, remember, and retrieve information obtained from service desks at shopping centers and malls, from information counters at railroad and bus terminals, and at the desks of receptionists. Teachers and trainers who wish to prepare their students for a successful and independent life in the community must provide them with many functional learning experiences designed to assist learners in understanding the oral communications from those they will likely encounter as they function actively on a daily basis in the multidimensional life of the community.

Written Comprehension

In addition to countless oral communications, individuals need to understand a large variety of written materials. They must be able to read and interpret words, phrases, sentences, and paragraphs. They must also respond appropriately to pictographs, rebuses, and markings on signs, labels, watches, clocks, measuring instruments, dials, and gauges. In the case of many dials, watches, clocks, measuring instruments, and gauges, one must also read the space between unnumbered or unlettered markings to determine what intervals are present, but undesignated. Among the written communications that individuals must respond to as they function on a daily basis are:

1. Written information found on street, traffic, bicyclist, and pedestrian signs (informative, warning/cautionary, and directing); clothing labels (size, cleaning instructions, and composition); price tags; food and package labels; signs on buildings, stores, and movie and theater marquees; signs directing action (exit, entrance, push, pull); signs that supply essential information (office hours, hours of operation, open, closed); and signs that indicate direction (arrows) or location (appearing on clothing racks and store shelves);
2. Written information in personal notes and letters;
3. Written information in business and work-related correspondence (work orders, inventory sheets);

4. Written information in menus, maps, charts, diagrams, graphs, figures, and tables;
5. Written information in directories and schedules;
6. Written information appearing on flyers, posters, billboards, and bulletin boards;
7. Written information on packages, vending and other machines, equipment (household and automobile), games, toys, and media and technological materials and equipment;
8. Written information in the many blanks and forms required by various agencies and organizations (library card applications, credit card applications, insurance policies, and tax forms);
9. Written information in newspapers, magazines, pamphlets, catalogs, and brochures and on television;
10. Written information on bills, work time cards, check stubs, market receipts, checks, deposit and withdrawal slips, and bank accounts.

Teachers and trainers who teach from a functional perspective must provide their students with learning experiences designed to assist them in developing the requisite knowledge and skills involved in understanding and utilizing the many sources of written material they will confront as they function in the real world.

Sample Instructional Plan 1

Topic Area: Comprehension: *Literal Level*
Designed by: Karen Curtis
Time Recommended: 45 Minutes

Background Information

The student's oral language comprehension is showing significant progress in the area of following simple one and two commands involving actions she is to carry out. She retains the command even when there has been a 1-minute delay in its required execution and when other conversation has intervened.

(continued)

Sample Instructional Plan 1 *(cont.)*

She is also able to restate the command in her words and describe it as a past action. She is still experiencing difficulty with identifying the main idea and supporting details of written instructions.

Annual Goal (or General Objective)

The student will comprehend the main idea and supporting details of written material (including diagrams) contained in manuals and brochures and in simple notes addressed to her.

Short-Term Instructional Objective

The student will correctly carry out simple directions found in packages and written on machinery, equipment, games, toys, packages, and items that are to be assembled.

Cognitive Dimensions

1. Identifying the main idea or purpose of a written message;
2. Comprehending the explicitly stated details;
3. Remembering the facts in sequence;
4. Articulating the facts in one's own words;
5. Applying the facts meaningfully.

Functional Context

The student will develop the skills involved in obtaining and responding appropriately to information found in reading materials she encounters in her environment, including: signs and labels, simple charts, diagrams, maps, menus, directories, and schedules.

Lesson Objective

When the student is given a diagram and written instructions for assembling a dollhouse, she will do so with minimal assistance from the teacher.

Materials and Equipment

1. Worktable;
2. Assembled dollhouse;
3. Dollhouse to be assembled;

(continued)

Sample Instructional Plan 1 *(cont.)*

4. Dollhouse furniture;
5. Self-developing camera.

Motivating Activity

Show the student a prototype of a fully assembled dollhouse. Tell her that she will assemble one just like it from the directions found in the package and then place dollhouse furniture in at least one room. Next show her the self-developing camera, and say, "When you have put together your dollhouse, we will take its picture and send it home for your parents to see."

Instructional Procedures

1. Show the student the assembled dollhouse. Encourage her to look at it carefully and examine it with her hands. Ask her to describe what she sees and to tell you what the object is and what people do with it.
2. Assist her, as necessary, in removing the unassembled dollhouse from its package. Tell her that she should find the directions so she can put her dollhouse together easily and successfully. Ask her to explain what "directions" are for and why they are important for putting things together properly. Once she has located the directions, ask her to read them to herself. Ask her to explain to you why the directions are placed in the package by the manufacturer.
3. Once she has read the assembly information, ask her to review it by stating each step in turn in her own words while she points to the diagram and to the parts of the dollhouse to be assembled.
4. After she has stated the process to be followed, tell her to proceed. Provide assistance and correction only when needed. Praise her at appropriate intervals.

Assessment Strategy

Listen to the student to see whether she:
1. Grasps the main idea that the purpose of the written direction was to help the purchaser assemble the dollhouse;
2. Identifies the sequence of actions in her own words and then follows them.

(continued)

Sample Instructional Plan 1 *(cont.)*

Follow-Up Activity or Objective

If the student achieves the lesson objective, proceed to assisting her in responding appropriately to key words found on employment forms and other simple blanks and forms.

Sample Instructional Plan 2

Topic Area: Comprehension: *Interpretive or Inferential Level*
Designed by: Albert De Gennaro
Time Recommended: 1 Hour

Background Information

The student is now able to read at the literal level when dealing with simple directions and information found in personal notes, directories, schedules, blanks, and forms.

Annual Goal (or General Objective)

The student will make inferences and draw conclusions using information gained at the literal level combined with prior knowledge to comprehend spoken and written material.

Short-Term Instructional Objective

The student will make appropriate decisions in diverse functional situations by correctly interpreting and making inferences about information found on various signs and labels.

Cognitive Dimensions

1. Comprehending spoken and written material at the literal level;

(continued)

Sample Instructional Plan 2 *(cont.)*

2. Making inferences;
3. Drawing conclusions;
4. Making judgments;
5. Generalizing;
6. Summarizing;
7. Comparing and contrasting;
8. Interpreting figurative language;
9. Solving problems;
10. Dealing with abstract ideas;
11. Utilizing information gained at the literal level combined with prior knowledge.

Functional Context

The student will make decisions in diverse functional situations based on information located on signs and labels found in the community.

Lesson Objective

When the student is shown representative warning and nonwarning signs he might encounter in his local community, he will describe the purpose of each sign, its basic meaning, and the appropriate action he should take to heed its underlying message.

Materials and Equipment

1. Teacher-made signs;
2. Teacher-made cautionary/warning sign chart;
3. Photographs of actual signs found in the community, showing not only the words but also the scene in which the sign is displayed or posted;
4. Self-developing camera.

Motivating Activity

After you have explored the community for representative signs, take the student for a walk over the same area. Join him in taking photographs of appropriate signs to be used in classroom activities. Ask him to talk about the ones he already understands.

(continued)

Sample Instructional Plan 2 *(cont.)*

Instructional Procedures

1. Show the student photographs of signs in his community that are not warning signs. For example, those that identify the names of buildings, stores, and places of interest as well as those signs and billboards advertising products. Ask him to explain why these signs are placed in the community and how he should respond to their messages. When there are signs for which he has had no previous experience, assist him in interpreting the purpose of the sign and in making judgments about the information found therein.

2. Next give him problems to solve in relation to the photographs of these community signs. For example, say to the student, "You are interested in going to see a basketball game. One of the signs advertises a basketball game. When are there scheduled basketball games? Where are they taking place? What teams are playing? What is the cost of admission? Based on the information on the sign, will you be able to go to one or more of the games according to your budget, transportation, and schedule?"

3. Then show him photographs of cautionary and warning signs found in his local community. Include signs, if appropriate to the community, such as : "No Trespassing," "Private Road," "Do Not Drink the Water," "No Picnicking," "Do Not Pick the Flowers," "Keep Off the Grass," "No Littering," "Beware of the Dog," "DANGER–CONSTRUCTION," "Emergency Door," "No Swimming," and "Pedestrians Prohibited." For each of the signs, ask him to explain what the words mean, what the person(s) who put up the sign wanted to warn or caution the reader about, what should he avoid doing, and what are the possible things that might happen to him if he did not "listen" to the sign. Those signs for which the student has had no previous experience must be discussed with him.

4. Next give him problems to solve in relation to the photographs of these community signs. For example, say to the student, "You are walking in your communnity and

(continued)

Sample Instructional Plan 2 *(cont.)*

come across this sign. What should you do and what shouldn't you do? Why and why not?"

5. Show him your teacher-made signs and ask him to tell you in his own words what these signs mean and how he should apply the information he gets from these signs to influence his behavior.
6. Lastly, show him the chart of warning signs and ask him to explain in his own words how the information in each notation is meant to assist him in monitoring his actions.

Assessment Strategy

Listen to the student as he states in his own words what was the reason or purpose of each sign. Observe if he makes appropriate inferences and interpretations based on the words, phrases, and sentences found there.

Follow-Up Activity or Objective

If the student achieves the lesson objective, proceed to a lesson in which he is expected to read, make inferences, draw conclusions, and summarize written information found in newspaper and magazine articles.

Sample Instructional Plan 3

Topic Area: Comprehension: *Critical Level*

Designed by: Howard Honig

Time Recommended: 1 Hour, 15 Minutes

Background Information

The student is now in a school-based transitioning program preparing her to leave the formal school setting and to partici-

(continued)

Sample Instructional Plan 3 (cont.)

pate more actively in the community, especially in terms of work, leisure-time pursuits, and general social interaction.

Annual Goal (or General Objective)

The student will make wise decisions concerning whether she should engage in diverse interpersonal, social, and leisure-time activities as well as financial transactions.

Short-Term Instructional Objective

The student will make appropriate decisions in diverse functional situations by correctly evaluating a speaker's purpose, mood, and authenticity in relation to the appropriateness and importance to her own needs, desires, and wants.

Cognitive Dimensions

1. Comprehending spoken and written material at the literal and interpretive/inferential levels;
2. Evaluating the author's or speaker's purpose, mood, and authenticity;
3. Identifying and validating the content presented, evaluating it based on previous knowledge and experience;
4. Making judgments on the possible consequences of participating or not participating in specific actions and suggested activities.

Functional Context

The student will make judicious decisions when confronted with disreputable characters who are engaging in various con game schemes.

Lesson Objective

When the student is confronted with several role plays involving con games, she will refuse to be conned. She will explain the

(continued)

Sample Instructional Plan 3 *(cont.)*

reasons based on her evaluation of the speaker, the validity of the content, and the importance of the "deal" to her own needs.

Materials and Equipment

1. Videotapes of legitimate television commercials;
2. Videotapes of televised scenes depicting someone engaging in a con game (for example, the television spot showing an unsavory character attempting to obtain someone's credit card number over the telephone);
3. Newspaper articles telling of incidents in which people were conned out of their money by falling for several different types of con games;
4. Newspaper and magazine advertisements, including those with a history of responsible merchandizing as well as those engaging in questionable tactics.

Motivating Activity

Ask the student whether she knows about any situations involving people who were cheated of their money by individual people, by articles in newspapers and magazines, and by advertisements that are mailed to the home or appear in newspapers and magazines. After the student has provided some examples, give some examples of your own.

Instructional Procedures

1. Show the student a videotape that you have developed exhibiting several reputable television commercials that depict people trying to sell something. Ask her whether she thinks the person in the commercial is getting paid for his or her work. Ask her to identify the reasons why she might want or might not want to buy an advertised product or service.
2. Next show the student a videotape that you have developed depicting people in public service and other television spots that depict individuals being exploited. Ask her to answer the following questions, "What do you think is the speaker's purpose?" "Why do you think he or she is saying what he or she is saying?" "What does the speaker

(continued)

Sample Instructional Plan 3 *(cont.)*

want from you?" "Is the information he or she is presenting truthful and honest?" "How can I verify it?" "Do I think
this is an honest person?" "Should I do what the speaker is asking me to do?" Provide assistance when needed in helping the
student respond to these questions.

3. Then give her copies of newspaper and magazine articles
   which report on con games. Ask her to read the articles to herself and then to tell you why the person in the article was
   fooled and what the person should have done to avoid being
   exploited.
4. Then show her advertisements from reputable sources,
   including those appearing in newspapers and magazines.
   Ask her to evaluate them in terms of their authenticity and
   in terms of her own needs and requirements. Then show
   her exploitive examples of advertisements and ask her to
   evaluate these.
5. Engage in several role plays in which you act the part of
   the "con person" and she is expected to reject your offer.

Assessment Strategy

Listen to the student to see whether she correctly identified and
evaluated the various con games, differentiating them from
reputable salespersons selling authentic products and services.

Follow-Up Activity or Objective

If the student achieves the instructional objective, proceed to a lesson in which she is expected to make judicious decisions in situations regarding sexual harassment or other types of exploitation.

Sample Instructional Plan 4

Topic Area: Comprehension: *Creative Level*
Designed by: Bernard Pine
Time Recommended: Two, 45-Minute Sessions

(continued)

Sample Instructional Plan 4 *(cont.)*

Background Information

The student is an intellectually gifted student with severe physical disabilities. He has been identified as having severe cerebral palsy of the athetoid type, is nonverbal, and requires some form of augmentative communication.

Annual Goal (or General Objective)

The student will participate in deciding the type of augmentative communication he will use and develop the skills to communicate as effectively and efficiently as possible, given the nature of his intelligence and the severity of his physical disability.

Short-Term Instructional Objective

The student will suggest options available to him in arriving at the most efficient and effective type of augmentative communication based on the idiosyncratic nature of his disability and appropriate to his communicative needs and desires.

Cognitive Dimensions

1. Comprehending spoken and written material at the literal, interpretive/inferential, and critical levels;
2. Evaluating his own needs, assets, and limitations;
3. Identifying existing options as potential solutions to the existing problem;
4. Arriving at additional or novel options that are potential solutions to the existing need.

Functional Context

The student will identify programming and resource options that are likely to assist him in meeting functional demands given the specific nature of his abilities and disabilities.

Lesson Objective

When the student is told about and given scientific articles to read concerning available augmentative devices and approaches,

(continued)

Sample Instructional Plan 4 *(cont.)*

he will communicate in his current manner (word processor) those options he believes are appropriate to his needs and condition. He will suggest other options or modifications in the devices for possible adaptations by appropriate professionals.

Materials and Equipment

1. Videotapes that demonstrate available augmentative devices and their use by students with physical disabilities;
2. Articles from scientific publications and advertisements that offer augmentative devices for persons who are nonverbal because of severe physical disability;
3. Newspaper articles that report on the successful use of augmentative equipment by persons with severe physical disability.

Motivating Activity

If available, ask a student with similar disabilities to demonstrate the use of his or her augmentative device. Show the videotape of several different devices as they are explained and demonstrated. Ask the student for his responses to what he has seen and heard.

Instructional Procedures

1. Discuss with the student several of the augmentative devices with which you are familiar. Show him advertisements, pictures, and articles from newspapers and scientific journals about these devices and their use. Give him time to read the articles and meet with him again for a second 45-minute session in which you discuss the various options available to him.
2. Encourage him to suggest modifications or other options that might better meet his individual needs.
3. Record his suggestions and assist him in locating possible sources for additional options and for exploration of resource people and companies that may assist him in obtaining the most effective and efficient device possible.

(continued)

Sample Instructional Plan 4 *(cont.)*

Assessment Strategy

Observe the student to see whether he has identified the various options that are realistically available to him, meet his communicative needs, and minimize his problems from his physical disabilities. Determine whether he has arrived at any novel options in his attempt to meet his individual needs and aspirations.

Follow-Up Activity or Objective

If the student achieves the lesson objective, proceed to a lesson in which he explores his other needs relevant to his special requirements arising from communicative needs and his physical limitations.

SUMMARY

The ability to comprehend is extremely important to the individual's survival and success, not only in the classroom but throughout life. All teachers and trainers should help students develop the ability to comprehend, because comprehension is the foundation for meaningful learning. Comprehension involves bridging the gap between what the student already knows and what he or she needs to learn. Memorizing words and isolated facts is not comprehension. All aspects of the language arts, listening, speaking, reading, and writing, should be included because the student's language facility forms the foundation for comprehension. Students must be provided with a wide variety of meaningful real-life activities that will enable them to build their comprehension ability.

6

CRITICAL THINKING

In the previous chapter on comprehension, the critical level was briefly discussed, but the various aspects of critical comprehension—application, analysis, synthesis, and evaluation—were not analyzed. This chapter examines these aspects in some detail by focusing on critical thinking, since critical comprehension involves critical thinking. Critical thinking is given special emphasis because it is extremely important for daily living, and yet it usually receives minimal emphasis in the overall school program.

It is difficult to think critically and not be creative at the same time. When the listener or reader analyzes and evaluates information, he or she almost invariably synthesizes relevant background experiences and the facts presented, in order to make judgments, decisions, or draw conclusions. The conclusions or decisions arrived at will of necessity be "new," since they reflect the individual's perception as seen through his or her background experiences. For the purpose of emphasis, however, critical thinking is dealt with separately in this chapter.

A RATIONALE FOR CRITICAL THINKING

In this century unprecedented and fateful social, economic, and political changes have taken place. Often these changes have occurred so rapidly that before one can understand or adjust to one situation, other changes occur. Rather than simplifying life, these changes have rendered it increasingly more complex and demanding. The result is that the individual is constantly challenged to deal with changes occurring too rapidly for him or her to absorb, while at the same time, reexamine and readjust his or her beliefs, values, goals, and needs to cope with the ever changing world order. Viewing the volatile state of society and the dilemma that the individual faces as he or she tries to come to terms with it, Romanish (1986) affirms, "Critical thinking *is essential* in a society in transition or in a state of change" [emphasis supplied] (p. 45). He further suggests that the qualitative and quantitative differences between past and present conditions of society resulting from the forces of change, "demand that the populace be equipped to understand, analyze, and respond in ways that are positive and productive on both individual and societal levels" (p. 46). He further states that young people must acquire the ability to critically judge and analyze situations that occur in their experiences and environments, in their daily lives as well as those that occur as they interact with the political, social, and economic institutions.

Devoid of the capacity to think critically, individuals may be extremely susceptible to dogmatism, deceptions, and the acceptance of irrational suggestions. If students are expected to function as responsible citizens of a democracy, both in their present state as children and later as adults, they must be empowered to analyze and evaluate the events taking place around them, especially those that impact directly on their lives. To ignore this important area of the individual's development is to minimize his or her ability to function effectively and productively in society. This lack also renders the student incapable of making the kinds of informed decisions necessary for his or her own benefit and for the good of society in general.

Researchers (Austin & Morrison, 1963) discovered that very little attention is given to critical thinking at the first and second grade levels of schools in the United States. More recent studies by the National Assessment of Educational Progress (1976) indicated that more than 50% of high school students were unable to make correct responses to questions requiring critical thinking. It is obvious that schools are not doing an effective job in helping students to think critically. This is very disturbing, because students' school years as well as the rest of their lives are and will be replete with circumstances that will demand every aspect of critical and creative thinking. Critical thinking skills are, perhaps, the most important of the comprehension skills, and yet are the least developed.

Education affords a crucial opportunity to assist students in developing critical awareness and competency. Since the school is a microcosm of the world, educators can discover, as well as provide, many opportunities to facilitate critical thinking. If the activities and methods used to develop critical thinking are meaningful and relevant to real life, hopefully, students will be able to make appropriate adaptations to meet the demands of adult life.

Romanish (1986) suggests two important reasons justifying the inclusion of critical thinking in the school curriculum. The first is that it endows and equips an individual with the ability to relate to the various dimensions of the world, comprehend it, and take part in it. The second justification has both political and social ramifications. An enlightened citizenry, equipped with the ability to think critically, will make informed critical judgments and decisions and eschew dogmatism and sloganeering. Education can and must provide concurrent ongoing enlightenment and the opportunity for students to become critical thinkers. Critical thinking is clearly a *necessity* in the education of students.

The ultimate goal of encouraging and developing students' critical thinking ability is to assist them in acquiring the competency to choose, discard, adapt, and use various types of information presented to them. Students must learn to evaluate not only the content of what they read and hear but also the form of presentation. As they do this, they must apply various criteria. Among these criteria are values—the individual's values which must be examined against those of the author or speaker. Alexander et al. (1983) suggests, "critical reading [listening] instruction must be involved with the student's competency in interrelating the values inherently put forth by reading materials with his own personal values. It may also relate to his awareness of his own values and how well he is able to put these aside while examining the values of others" (p. 184). There are many values, and people's value systems differ. To help students deal with the conflicts that may arise as they make value judgments or decisions, instructors need to provide many direct and vicarious experiences that will demonstrate how conflicts are resolved and decisions are made when values are involved. Instructors should also provide students with activities that will give students lots of practice in dealing appropriately with their values and the values of others and in demonstrating the importance and relationship between values and judgments to be made.

It is impossible for any teacher to completely prepare students to deal critically with every situation, subject, or topic they will encounter in their present or future circumstances. Additionally, no one has acquired, or is able to acquire sufficient knowledge and experiences necessary to make critical analyses of all subjects or topics, whether one encounters these areas of information through reading or listening. Knowledge has increased phenomenally in every field, and no one is expected to know all there is to know in any one subject, let alone all subjects. It is imperative, however, that educators assist students in developing skills and attitudes of awareness and inquiry necessary to analyze, evaluate, and verify content; detect unsupported statements, broad generalizations, and incorrect conclusions drawn in the absence of substantiated data; and locate and use a variety of resources to ascertain the validity of information (Harris & Smith, 1980).

DEFINING CRITICAL THINKING?

For decades, educators have been wrestling with definitions of critical thinking. In 1910, John Dewey wrote, *How We Think*, and since then other researchers have offered various descriptions of critical thinking. D'Angelo (1971) states that, "Critical thinking is the process of evaluating statements, arguments, and experiences" (p. 7). Later, he suggested that when one evaluates, one's attitudes and skills are involved. McPeck (1981), on the other hand, suggests that, "On the surface at least, perhaps the most notable characteristic of critical thought is that it involves a certain skepticism, or suspension of assent, toward a given statement, established norm or mode of doing things" (p. 6). Arendt (1977) describes critical thinking as a quest for meaning rather than mere acquisition of knowledge. Beyer (1984) defines critical thinking as problem solving along with such basic thought operations as recall and synthesis. Despite these attempts at defining critical thinking, no one knows exactly what occurs as one thinks critically. Collahan and Corvo (1980) note that there is still no comprehensive definition of critical thinking. The consensus, however, is that there are certain skills and abilities that constitute critical thinking. Ennis (1962) delineates 12 such skills and abilities: (1) obtaining the meaning of a statement, (2) deciding whether the author's [speaker's] line of reasoning is ambiguous, (3) deciding whether there is contradiction between or among statements, (4) judging whether a conclusion can necessarily be drawn, (5) deciding whether a statement is sufficiently specific, (6) deciding if a statement is indeed relevant to a specific principle, (7) judging the reliability of an observation, (8) deciding if a conclusion drawn from a generalization is justified, (9) deciding if a problem has been recognized, (10) deciding whether a statement is an assumption or a fact, (11) deciding if a definition is satisfactory, and (12) judging the authenticity and the acceptability of a statement.

Russell (1956) succinctly outlines four criteria that are necessary for critically analyzing materials. He suggests that an individual must have: (1) some prior knowledge of the subject with which he or she is dealing, (2) an attitude of inquiry and a willingness to suspend judgment until all facts have been examined, (3) the ability to apply methods of logic and analysis to the information, and (4) the ability to make judgments on the basis of analysis.

As inclusive as these lists seem to be, they do not fully describe all that occurs as one engages in critical thinking. Nor is it possible to prescribe a list of skills which, if mastered, will ensure that one will become a critical thinker. After having employed his rather comprehensive list, Ennis (1962), himself, concedes that, "Complete criteria cannot be established for critical thinking" (p. 85). Moreover, the ability to use all the skills listed above does not necessarily mean that one is a critical thinker. Nor does it mean that one has to utilize all of the above skills every time one processes oral or written information to be considered a critical thinker.

Educators must not conceptualize critical thinking as merely a set of discrete skills students must master. Embracing this view, educators will fail to provide the climate, freedom, encouragement, materials, and opportunities necessary for students to become critical thinkers.

In its broadest sense, and for the purpose of this text, critical thinking may be defined as the ability to apply relevant criteria to analyze, evaluate, make judgments on, and synthesize information already understood at the literal and interpretive levels. It also involves the ability to apply ideas learned in one situation to a new or related situation. Literal and interpretive comprehension are crucial to critical thinking, because a clear understanding of the author's or speaker's main ideas and points of view is necessary before one can make an appropriate analysis or evaluation of the ideas presented.

The reader or listener's background experiences, concepts, and prior knowledge which form his or her schemata are also essential to critical thinking. These schemata form the basis for developing and using the relevant criteria necessary to make judgments concerning the author or speaker's purpose, whether the information is fact or opinion, the authenticity of the materials, and the validity of claims made. Robinson (1964) says to read critically, one must have the ability to apply pertinent criteria to evaluate the "veracity, validity, and worth of what is read, based on criteria or standards developed through experience" (p. 3). This observation also applies to information which one processes auditorially.

Another important facet of critical thinking is the ability to reason logically and objectively, making sure to suspend judgment until one has clearly understood the content and has examined it from as many angles as possible. Roe et al. (1991) affirm, "Readers, [listeners] should test the author's [speaker's] assertions against their own observations, information, and logic" (p. 85). Students should be encouraged to ask questions constantly as they read or listen to the ideas of others before they draw conclusions or make decisions. Questions such as the following will guide them in making informed judgments about what they hear or read: "What is the author or speaker's purpose?" "Does he or she want to inform me, instruct me, entertain me, persuade me, or con me?" "What mental posture should I assume to deal with the author or speaker's purpose(s)?" "Are his or her claims verifiable?" "Is the information fact or opinion?" "Is he or she trustworthy?" "Does he or she overuse emotionally loaded language?" and "Are my personal reservations or biases affecting my logic and objectivity?"

Wolf, Huck, & King (1967) suggest that there are three major types of competencies involved in processing written [and also oral] information critically. The first deals with *semantics*. Students must be competent in comprehending the denotative as well as the connotative meaning of words. Often the speaker or writer's messages are couched in connotative rather than denotative meanings of the words and phrases that they use. Students who rely solely on the denotative meaning will, therefore, miss much of the communication and, consequently, will not be able to make correct analyses or evaluations of the ideas presented. Students must also recognize and understand words that are used in an obscure, imprecise, persuasive, or emotional manner.

The second important competency is *logic*. This involves the ability to: judge the reliability of facts and the line of reasoning, detect and interpret persuasive techniques, and distinguish facts from opinions or fallacies. Finally, students must be competent in judging *authenticity*. They must be able to determine whether or not the author or speaker is qualified in a particular area(s) and whether sufficient information has been provided to support the claims presented. Students must also be capable of locating and using other resources to verify authenticity.

THE FOUR ASPECTS OF CRITICAL THINKING

Critical thinking involves four aspects: application, analysis, synthesis, and evaluation. It is often quite difficult to separate these aspects of critical thinking, because they overlap and are interrelated. In making applications, for instance, one has to make evaluations and also synthesize. However, for the purpose of emphasis and clarity, each of these aspects is discussed separately in this chapter.

Application

A very important skill that students need to develop in order to think critically about what they read or hear is the ability to transfer information or ideas already acquired to new situations and new relationships. Without this ability, critical thinking, or learning in general, would be limited. Students demonstrate their understanding of a generalization or a principle when they are able to apply it to new information. Students may be asked to solve a problem, modify a product or operation, or develop a new item by using previous knowledge. In making applications, students are required to use information previously learned in situations which are different from the ones in which the material was learned. Often the student cannot rely on the content or context in which the original learning occurred to solve the problem. Rather, he or she must understand the relationship of the generalization or principle previously learned and the new situation to which the application must be made.

Analysis

Analysis involves the ability to process information by distinguishing among facts, opinions, hypotheses, and assumptions. At the analysis level, students examine relationships among ideas and compare and contrast information. Lamberg and Lamb (1980) suggest several different kinds of analyses: (1) Students may analyze components of the text. For example, students may differentiate conclusions from supporting statements, facts from opinions, and explicit from implied statements. (2) Students may analyze relationships among ideas. For example, they can identify cause-and-effect and comparison-and-contrast relationships and sequence. (3) They may also examine the structure and the intent of the information. For example, they may identify the author or speaker's purpose and the techniques that the information-giver uses to express his or her views.

Analysis represents the steps the reader or listener takes to understand how the author or speaker develops, constructs, and presents his or her ideas. While doing so, the individual receiving the information manipulates the presentation by asking questions such as: "What is the main idea?" "What are the major details?" "How do the details relate to the main idea?" "Is sufficient information provided?" and "Are the author or speaker's ideas coherent?"

Instructors can assist students in learning to examine various types of information analytically by modeling and also by providing them with many activities and opportunities which demand analysis.

Synthesis

A synthesis task requires students to combine different aspects of ideas from various sources into a new coherent form. Students may be asked to combine various parts of information to arrive at a new solution or to find unique solutions to some unfamiliar problems. The key word in synthesis is "new." The student's response may not be original in the sense that no one else has ever made that response before. If, however, the student's response represents an original way in which the student organizes or views his or her experience, the response may be considered "new" (Roe et al., 1991). Students may, for example, present a new variation on a piece of music or a play which illustrates a new view of interpreting the play or piece of music. Students may also arrive at a new solution to an existing problem.

Teachers and trainers can encourage and help students develop synthesis ability by providing activities and situations which demand the use of synthesis skills such as gathering and using information from various sources to defend a position or disprove a statement. They may also be asked to examine various recipes and use information from several of them to create a new recipe.

Evaluation

Evaluation represents the highest level of critical thinking. This involves applying criteria or standards to make judgments on content and other aspects of a presentation. Criteria are critical to making relevant judgments about ideas, methods, products, or people. Evaluation is not a quick, subjective judgment made in the absence of facts. It depends on the individual's ability to understand literal and interpretive ideas and also to appraise the veracity and validity of materials. In making judgments, the individual must apply both internal criteria developed from background experiences and external criteria which may be from other individuals or sources.

The student may experience difficulty in applying criteria to make judgments when his or her internal criteria such as values, beliefs, and assumptions conflict with criteria from external sources such as the text's or speaker's ideas (Harris & Smith, 1980). It is the teacher's responsibility to assist students in developing objectivity and some level of detachment from their own views and biases as they examine and clarify the assumptions they have and deal with external criteria. Teachers also need to help students to understand that valid judgments should be made on the basis of having adequate information and also by considering information from various viewpoints.

All the levels discussed above are integrated, interrelated aspects of critical thinking and must be taught as such. Teachers and trainers should not attempt to present these aspects in a disjointed manner. The aim should be to assist students in becoming competent critical thinkers.

TEACHING FOR CRITICAL THINKING

Many school curricula claim to provide for the development of students' critical thinking. Yet, in reality only a few do. Many teachers and trainers fail to develop students' critical thinking abilities because they believe that there is not enough time in the schedule to do so, or because they fail to devote enough time for students to learn to think. Some instructors also believe that critical thinking has to be taught as a separate subject rather than as an integral part of every subject. These instructors miss countless excellent opportunities during the daily activities of the class to encourage, model, and foster critical thinking. There are also those teachers who are reluctant to encourage students to think critically, because they are afraid that giving students the freedom to analyze, question, and judge authority figures, such as teachers and authors of texts, may threaten their control of the students and the learning situation and challenge their competence. Another contributing factor to teachers' neglect in guiding students to think critically is that these teachers and trainers themselves were not taught to think critically.

Romanish (1986) suggests that there are many other impediments to the development of critical thinking. He lists the following: (1) the fallacy that only the talented and gifted students can or should learn to think critically; (2) current goals of schools are concerned primarily with socialization and uniformity, which does not allow for the development of critical thought; (3) the fact that the current system is preoccupied mainly with those aspects of the curriculum which can be standardized and tested; (4) a misconception that critical thinking ability can be developed and measured in a hurry; (5) obsession with obtaining "correct" answers to teachers' questions; (6) overcrowded classes—in such classes students do not have opportunities to dialogue sufficiently with one another; (7) the school and society, in general, place little value on critical thinking; (8) the experiences and activities that school provide are artificial rather than relevant to real life; and (9) students are not allowed freedom to be independent learners and thinkers.

Those instructors who try to infuse critical thinking into the subjects they teach, discover that it is not as esoteric and technically formidable as might appear. Teaching for critical thinking means that teachers, administrators, and other adults in the school environment should create conditions that stimulate and encourage inquiry, trust, divergent responses, risk taking, speculation, problem solving, and creativity. Beyer (1983) suggests that instructors can do much to ensure their success in teaching students to think critically by attending to three important components: "1) The learning environment, 2) strategies and methods used to instruct, and 3) the coordination and structure of [thinking] skill teaching throughout the entire curriculum." These factors, he further suggests, "are the foundations of effective instruction in thinking skills at all grade levels K–12 and beyond" (p. 44). A supportive learning environment which allows students the time and freedom to interact with other students, to research and invent, and in which the teacher operates as a facilitator rather than as an information dispenser, is essential to the development of critical thinking. This does not mean, however, that there is no place for direct instruction which will enable students to master critical thinking and in learning to apply these skills meaningfully in and out of the classroom. Direct, systematic, and effective instruction is a crucial part of building critical thinking.

There are many things that teachers and trainers can do to help students develop the ability to think critically. They can supplement class textbooks and other in-school materials with real-life materials such as: various kinds of oral and written advertisements; brochures for travel, entertainment, and various products; product labels; newspaper articles, especially those from the feature sections; the advertising sections of newspapers and other periodicals; catalogs; videotapes of various types of advertisements and documentaries; and credit card and lease contracts, as well as other materials that students are likely to encounter in their adult lives.

Students should also be given time and freedom to think, discuss, and question oral and written information. They may do so in large or small groups or in entire class discussions. Teachers and trainers may provide students with questions, or they may encourage students to preview the materials and then make up their own questions, which will help them analyze and evaluate the content. Teachers should expect and accept some open-ended and divergent answers to their questions. They should also teach students that a question may have more than one right answer and that they must analyze and evaluate other students' answers before making judgments on them. Students do not automatically develop the ability to think critically, nor do they learn to do so because teachers and trainers constantly admonish them to "think." Educators must make a deliberate effort to plan and implement programs at all levels of learning to enable students to become critical thinkers.

As was stated earlier, critical thinking is given little emphasis in the classroom. When it does receive some attention, however, it is not made applicable to real-life situations, and students are usually only asked to circle right or wrong answers. If critical thinking is given such little emphasis in regular classrooms, it is very possible that in mainstreamed classrooms and special classes it is not given any attention. Many people who deal with special students have the misguided and unfortunate idea that these students cannot think, and, therefore, they do not need to be taught to make applications, to analyze, to evaluate, or to synthesize. This self-fulfilling prophecy further incapacitates the very students who need the most assistance in making decisions based on the critical evaluation of information.

Teachers and trainers should not deny students with learning problems the opportunity to develop the ability to think critically, because these students live in the same real world and deal with decision-making situations as do all other students. Very often these special students are the individuals on whom dishonest and unscrupulous people prey. Instructors should not think that only those students with average or above ability need to or can learn to think critically.

Another important consideration is that all learning is developmental. Students do not acquire any skill overnight, nor can they reach the highest level of competency or performance before they are cognitively ready. This does not mean that students should not be taught at the particular level of understanding at which they are operating. Students at all levels should be provided with the opportunity to develop their ability to think critically. It is a mistake to think that students in the lower grades cannot and should not be taught to think critically. This is an unfortunate and incorrect assumption, because during all stages of their lives, all students are faced with and will face situations in which they must make decisions based on their ability to analyze, evaluate, and make judgments on what they are told or what they read. These decisions may range from the 6-year-old simply deciding whether he or she should steal the cookie from the other child's lunch box or go to the pond to swim against mom's command not to, to the preteen or teenager's weighing the consequences of taking drugs or breaking into someone's home because a friend said it was "cool" to do so.

All students *can* be taught and *should* be taught to develop critical thinking skills at the level at which they are operating. Research (Covington, 1967; McCullough, 1957) has indicated that even those students in the lower elementary grades who were reading up to 2 years below grade level were able to read critically at their level. Simple questions like the following may be asked to initiate critical thinking: "Do you believe what you read or heard? Why do or don't you?" "Do you think that could really happen? Why or why not?" and "Do you like the story? Why or why not? How would you change it?" Questions may be asked at more complex levels to match the student's level of cognitive development.

Before students are asked to deal critically with written materials or oral information, teachers and trainers must assist them in understanding the various techniques that writers, advertisers, and people in general, use to motivate or persuade other people to do what they want them to do. Students must be taught how to detect the author or speaker's purpose and the kind of propaganda technique the communicator is using. Teachers must provide students with much practice in spotting signal words and phrases—such as "on the other hand," "however," "in addition," "on the contrary," and "but"—as well as emotionally loaded words and phrases such as "better than," "the best," "the only one," "everyone," "good people," "best loved," "most used," and many other such words and phrases that are used to persuade or pressure one to make decisions. Hopefully, with such help as instruction, guidance, and practice, students will develop the habit of questioning, analyzing, and evaluating what they read or hear before they make judgments or decisions.

THE FUNCTIONAL APPROACH TO THE DEVELOPMENT OF CRITICAL THINKING

As stated earlier, schools are apparently doing an inadequate job in helping students, especially those with disabilities, to think critically. This unfortunate situation is especially disconcerting if one views the curriculum from a functional perspective. It is clear that throughout the school years and increasingly in their adult life when they will be expected to be increasingly independent, students will have to make wise judgments, arrive at logical and well-conceived decisions, and draw rational conclusions about many factors pertinent to all areas of their lives.

When one is designing and implementing a critical thinking curriculum from a functional perspective, it is necessary to deal with real-life materials, especially those that attempt to persuade one to purchase various items and to influence one's values and behaviors. This is true whether these materials are legitimate advertisements, "con" games, or appeals to baser elements such as ethnic and racial hatred and prurient interests. For example, students must be assisted in critically examining oral and written advertisements, labels appearing on diverse products, and brochures that attempt to induce the reader to participate in travel and other leisure activities and to purchase various goods. Students must also be assisted in critically reviewing "hate" and "revisionist" literature disseminated by racist and other destructive groups and individuals. Special students and their family members must be assisted in this area, as they are more likely to be victimized by false advertisements, cure and treatment claims by charlatans and quacks, and other dangerous, dishonest, and exploitive people and tactics.

Teachers and trainers must also provide students with experiences designed to assist these individuals in making judgments, arriving at decisions, and drawing conclusions about dangerous and threatening situations involving natural phenomena such as when there are reports and warnings of possible earthquakes, floods, and adverse weather conditions such as tornadoes, hurricanes, or snowstorms. Additionally, students need assistance in dealing with potentially dangerous situations in which they are more likely to become victims. They need to make critical judgments involving safety factors such as refraining from hitchhiking, avoiding unsafe neighborhoods, refusing to ride in an automobile with an intoxicated driver, and refraining from venturing into unlit areas with inadequate security and surveillance.

Students must also be assisted in dealing with information provided by one-issue and other advocacy groups that attempt to convince readers or listeners to support a zealously pursued position. In cases such as this, students must be helped to reason logically and objectively, to suspend judgment, to examine the issue from as many different angles as possible, to consider different viewpoints, and to examine their own value system. Students often will be challenged by others to become advocates or to take a stand on diverse problems and issues that confront people in such areas as political, social, religious, or personal matters. Youngsters need to be alert to the existence of undesirable groups that promote causes that harm and that seek to alienate others. Students will have to judge whether they wish to take a stand on an issue, whether to financially support an advocacy group, or whether to become actively involved and committed to a particular group.

Each day of one's life, one is exhorted, expected, or required to make decisions. One is expected to make decisions in a wide range of situations; for example, the basics such as health, diet, and exercise; social and interpersonal relationships; avoidance of toxic and addictive elements; the selection of appropriate and affordable recreational activities; and the reasoned involvement in financial, social, and political matters. Instructors also must provide students with direct and simulated experiences that not only help them to meet the daily and weekly requirements of life but also in making long-range plans that will affect individuals in the future, such as planning for retirement.

Sample Instructional Plan 1

Topic Area: Critical Thinking: Application

Designed by: Kim Hall

Time Recommended: 1 1/2 Hours

Background Information

Despite the absence of a physical disability and the ability to walk with a satisfactory posture, the student frequently walks in an awkward manner. In addition, his hair is frequently untidy and his clothing is often disheveled. He also has a problem with personal hygiene in that he, on occasion, has an offensive body odor.

Annual Goal (or General Objective)

The student will groom himself and otherwise behave in ways that increase his ability to acquire and maintain friendships and to engage in successful dating practices.

Short-Term Instructional Objective

The student will groom himself satisfactorily and maintain walking and standing postures that will not draw undue attention to him and will make him more acceptable to peers.

Cognitive Dimensions

1. Comprehending and remembering the main ideas and supporting details that were explicitly stated;
2. Translating what he has seen and heard in his own words;
3. Making inferences;
4. Reasoning logically, drawing conclusions, making judgments, and generalizing;
5. Comparing and contrasting;
6. Solving problems and dealing with abstract ideas;
7. Analyzing, critiquing, and summarizing;
8. Applying prior knowledge to a new situation.

(continued)

Sample Instructional Plan 1 *(cont.)*

Functional Context

The student will prepare for a date and conduct himself appropriately when on a date.

Lesson Objective

When asked to prepare for a date, the student will groom himself and then engage in a role play in which he carries on a conversation with a female classmate while they are enjoying a snack.

Materials and Equipment

1. Table and two ice cream parlor chairs;
2. Deodorant, soap, hairbrush, comb, washcloth, and towels;
3. Change of clothing (clean but casual);
4. Video cassette with two segments depicting two versions (the right way and the wrong way) of two teenagers (preferably classmates) on a casual date at a fast food restaurant;
5. Video player, film, video camera, and a television monitor;
6. Pictures showing teenagers in different types of clothing, for example: formal, casual, work clothes, swimsuits, outfits for winter sports, and lounging clothes (robes and pajamas);
7. Snack such as ice cream sundaes.

Motivating Activity

Show the student pictures of teenagers taken from newspapers and magazines. These pictures should depict different articles of clothing appropriate to the pictures' content—that is, a teenager at the beach wearing a swimsuit and a teenager at a formal affair wearing a suit and tie. Engage the student in a discussion of the proper clothes to wear for different occasions.

(continued)

Sample Instructional Plan 1 *(cont.)*

Instructional Procedures

1. Engage the student in a discussion on the topic: "What can each of us do to help us acquire and keep friends and make us more attractive to the opposite sex?" or "What do teenagers look for in others when they decide that that person might be someone to date?" Start the discussion by talking about unpleasant body odor and how it is a "turn-off" to friends *and* romantic interests alike. Respond appropriately to his ideas and, whenever necessary, ask leading questions that elicit appropriate responses. In the conversation, cover all areas of grooming as well as the issue of standing, sitting, and walking postures.

2. Show him the videotape of two teenagers (preferably taken of two of his classmates) on a casual date at a fast food restaurant. Before showing the videotape, explain that there are two separate segments (the right way and the wrong way). Ask him to watch the film carefully so that he will be able to comment on how the teen subjects were dressed, the way they walked and sat, and the nature of their conversation.

3. After his analysis of the two segments of the film, tell him that you are going to make a video of him and a classmate on a pretend date. Explain that this film will have only one segment, *the right way to "look" and behave.* Show him the grooming materials, and ask him to tell you which ones he would use to prepare for the date. If appropriate, ask him to use the grooming materials and to change into the clean clothing. Then, tell him to talk to his date before the camera rolls to decide on topics they are going to discuss in their conversation while they are eating their snack.

4. Hold a rehearsal and correct any problems in posture, in grooming, and with the conversation. After the rehearsal, film the scene, show it to the "actors," and ask him and his date to critique it. After the critique, reshoot the scene to illustrate the improvements.

(continued)

Sample Instructional Plan 1 *(cont.)*

Assessment Strategy

Listen to the student to ascertain what behaviors he identified as being "turn-offs" to friends and prospective dates. Observe him to see whether he has groomed himself appropriately and had an acceptable posture. Listen to his comments on viewing the video cassette of his classmates and listen to his critique of his own performance. Record your observations on the Diagnostic Checklist.

Follow-Up Activity or Objective

If the student achieves the lesson objective, proceed to a lesson on cutting and cleaning his fingernails.

Sample Instructional Plan 2

Topic Area: Critical Thinking: Analysis
Designed by: Nicholas Smith
Time Recommended: 45 Minutes

Background Information

The student is experiencing problems in interpreting the body language of others and in realizing that the behavior of others is often caused by her own actions. She especially becomes alarmed when others become angry or upset, without realizing that the actions of others may be related, at times, to her own behavior.

(continued)

Sample Instructional Plan 2 *(cont.)*

Annual Goal (or General Objective)

The student will behave in ways that will result in positive reactions from peers and adults in her environment.

Short-Term Instructional Objective

The student will identify behaviors that are likely to get positive reactions from others and those actions or behaviors that will likely result in negative reactions from others.

Cognitive Dimensions

1. Comprehending and remembering the main ideas and supporting details that were explicitly stated;
2. Translating what she has seen and heard in her own words;
3. Making inferences;
4. Reasoning logically, drawing conclusions, making judgments, and generalizing;
5. Comparing and contrasting;
6. Solving problems and dealing with abstract ideas;
7. Analyzing and summarizing;
8. Distinguishing among facts;
9. Identifying cause and effect.

Functional Context

The student is having difficulty in establishing a responsive and rewarding environment. In her conversations with her teacher and speech pathologist, she often laments that she has no friends and that no one likes her. A major goal then is to help her to act in ways that will assist her in getting others to like her, to want to be in her company, and to obtain those behaviors and tangible items and rewards she desires.

Lesson Objective

When the student is asked to identify cause and effect relationships involving behaviors that make others happy, angry, and

(continued)

Sample Instructional Plan 2 *(cont.)*

upset, she will do so. She will also discuss how she must monitor and modify her behavior if she hopes to obtain positive reactions from the peers and adults in her life. She will practice these behaviors in a role play in which she is expected to demonstrate different behaviors that will lead to positive reactions.

Materials and Equipment

1. Photographs of peers and adults in her environment that depict happiness and anger;
2. Specially prepared video cassette of scenes from popular television shows, depicting cause-and-effect events;
3. Video cassette of peers and adults in her environment depicting scenes in which they react to the behavior of a student "actor" by appropriately showing happiness or anger. These emotions will be expressed in both speech and action. For example, the peers and adults in the tape will express anger by refusing to join the offending student "actor" in a leisure-time activity, or they will express happiness or delight by inviting the pleasant student "actor" to join them for lunch;
4. Video player and a television monitor;
5. Food items for a class lunch.

Motivating Activity

Show the student a specially prepared video of scenes taped from several popular television shows. These scenes should illustrate cause-and-effect relationships in which an actor causes positive and negative reactions in others (reactors). Discuss the show, the characters, the specific events, and the cause-and-effect sequence.

Instructional Procedures

1. Show the student photographs of peers and adults in her environment that illustrate happiness or anger. Ask the student to identify the emotion and to provide reasons why the person in the photograph might be happy, upset, or angry. After she has provided reasons for the

(continued)

Sample Instructional Plan 2 *(cont.)*

reactions depicted in the photographs and you have offered some examples from your own life, ask her to give you examples of how her own behavior caused positive and negative reactions from others.

2. Then, show the student the video of her peers and adults reacting to a student "actor" who is behaving in ways that lead to positive and negative reactions. Ask her to describe what she saw and heard and to explain why the positive reactions of others are preferable to negative ones.

3. Next, engage her in a discussion in which she addresses the questions: "What makes people happy, upset, and angry?" *and* "What do people do for or to others who make them happy, upset, or angry?" *and* "What she can do to change her behavior so that she will more likely get positive reactions and rewards from others?"

4. Finally, engage her in a role play in which she practices as many different ways as possible to make you happy. Reward her by preparing a special lunch and inviting her to share it with you.

Assessment Strategy

Listen to the student to determine whether she has correctly identified: behaviors that will cause negative and positive reactions from others; the way people behave when they are pleased, upset, or angry; and the ways she can change her behavior to get positive responses and rewards from others. Record her performance on the Diagnostic Checklist.

Follow-Up Activity or Objective

If the student achieves the lesson objective, proceed to a lesson in which she is expected to read and interpret articles in the local newspaper that illustrate cause-and-effect relationships.

(continued)

Sample Instructional Plan 3 *(cont.)*

Topic Area: Critical Thinking: Synthesis
Designed by: David Rodriques
Time Recommended: 45 Minutes

Background Information

The student has been participating in the sex education part of the functional curriculum. She has little prior information on this subject as evidenced by many naive comments and misinformation that she has offered in class discussions. Despite her age (14), she has already experienced substantial physical development and, consequently, appears to be much older than she is. She is, therefore, more likely to be sexually exploited.

Annual Goal (or General Objective)

The student will develop those critical thinking skills that will reduce the likelihood that she will be exploited by others.

Short-Term Instructional Objective

The student will describe the process of conception and discuss various birth control practices.

Cognitive Dimensions

1. Comprehending and remembering the main ideas and supporting details that were explicitly stated;
2. Translating what she has seen and heard in her own words;
3. Making inferences;
4. Reasoning logically, drawing conclusions, making judgments, and generalizing;
5. Comparing and contrasting;
6. Solving problems and dealing with abstract ideas;
7. Analyzing and summarizing;
8. Distinguishing among facts;

(continued)

Sample Instructional Plan 3 *(cont.)*

9. Identifying cause and effect;
10. Combining different ideas from different sources into a new form or new view

Functional Context

The student needs to separate fact from fiction and avoid being victimized and otherwise exploited by others in her environment. Her parents have also been alerted to the need to deal realistically with her sexual education, as part of their counseling and training sessions.

Lesson Objective

While participating in a role play, the student will avoid the sexual advances of a "date" by disproving a false statement made by him and by refusing to be exploited sexually.

Materials and Equipment

1. Newspaper and magazine articles about date rape;
2. Audio cassette of the school nurse or a physician discussing the conception process: fact and fiction;
3. Audio cassette player;
4. Video player and a television monitor;
5. Reference book on sex education, for example, *How Babies Are Made* (Time-Life Books).

Motivating Activity

Give the student copies of newspaper and magazine articles that deal with date rape. After she has had an opportunity to review them, engage her in a discussion on the issues and the implications she draws for her own behavior.

Instructional Procedures

1. Ask the student to tell you what she knows about the conception process. Encourage her to tell you any of the

(continued)

Sample Instructional Plan 3 *(cont.)*

false ideas that people have now or may have had in the past. If appropriate, tell her the myth that a woman can become pregnant from sitting in a chair that a man had just sat on.

2. Then, play the audio cassette of the school nurse or a physician discussing the facts and myths of the conception process. Make certain that the myth that "the first time cannot lead to pregnancy" is included in the presentation. Ask the student to tell in her own words what she has learned from listening to the cassette.

3. Next, show the student the reference book being used in the lesson. Direct her to the section that deals with the myths and facts of the conception process.

4. Finally, engage her in a role play in which her date tries to convince her to "Go all the way since you can't get pregnant the first time you do it!" Before the role play begins, tell her that her role requires that she avoids being exploited or victimized by her date. Videotape the role play and ask her to review what occurred. Reward her for disproving her date's statement. If she failed to do so, review the relevant information and redo the role play.

Assessment Strategy

Listen to the student to determine whether she used the information from the audio cassette, the newspapers and magazines, and the reference book to refute the statement made by her date and refused to be sexually exploited. Record her performance on the Diagnostic Checklist.

Follow-Up Activity or Objective

If the student achieves the lesson objective, proceed to a lesson in which she discusses birth control options and the pros and cons of birth control and the different available methods.

(continued)

Sample Instructional Plan 4 *(cont.)*

Topic Area: Critical Thinking: Evaluation

Designed by: Anna Maria Da Costa

Time Recommended: 1 Hour

Background Information

The student, as part of his transitioning program, has been working on those functional skills pertinent to his becoming a wise consumer of goods and services. He was sent on several shopping trips to explore his shopping behaviors. While he follows his previously prepared shopping list, he purchases items without regard to value, does not check the prices as shown on the register, and does not verify his change.

Annual Goal (or General Objective)

The student will develop those critical thinking skills that will assist him in becoming a wise consumer of goods and services.

Short-Term Instructional Objective

The student, when purchasing food, will purchase needed food in stores where he will obtain the best value for his money.

Cognitive Dimensions

1. Comprehending and remembering the main ideas and supporting details that were explicitly stated;
2. Translating what she has seen and heard in her own words;
3. Making inferences;
4. Reasoning logically, drawing conclusions, making judgments, and generalizing;
5. Comparing and contrasting;
6. Solving problems and dealing with abstract ideas;
7. Analyzing and summarizing;
8. Distinguishing among facts;
9. Appraising the veracity and validity of materials;
10. Applying internal criteria from prior experiences and external criteria in making judgments.

(continued)

Sample Instructional Plan 4 *(cont.)*

Functional Context

The student, in order to function successfully in his soon to be independent living community residence and with his limited income, must become a skillful comparative shopper.

Lesson Objective

When asked to review store flyers and newspaper advertisements for supermarkets in his area, he will make hypothetical shopping lists for at least two of these stores, based on his budget and a simulated weekly menu.

Materials and Equipment

1. Newspaper advertisements and flyers from local supermarkets;
2. Video cassette of commercials advertising various food products;
3. Video player and a television monitor;
4. Pad and pencils;
5. Budget sheet;
6. Food packages for two separate food items, representing different brands and including a store or generic brand.

Motivating Activity

Show the student a specially prepared video of television commercials that are advertising food items that the student likes. Be sure to include commercials that purport to include "real" people rather than celebrities or spokespersons. Ask him to evaluate the speaker's purpose and authenticity. Join him in a discussion of the nature of advertising and of propaganda in general.

Instructional Procedures

1. Having ascertained the student's food preferences, give him several different brands of at least two food items that can be tasted directly from the package without cooking and that are advertised in flyers and newspaper advertisements of local supermarkets. Without identi-

(continued)

Sample Instructional Plan 4 (cont.)

fying the brands (including a store or generic brand), ask him to select the one that he prefers in terms of taste, visual appeal, and other pertinent criteria. At this point, give him flyers and newspaper advertisements for local supermarkets. If he indicates a preference for one choice, ask him to look for this brand in the advertisements you have given him. Tell him to compare the prices for this item at the various stores. If he does not have a preference for any brand, ask him to compare the prices of all the brands that he has tested on the various flyers and advertisements you have given him.

2.   Then, give the student a copy of a hypothetical, yet realistic, weekly budget. Ask him to identify the amount of money available to purchase food. Explain that he has been on a long vacation trip and that his refrigerator and pantry are empty. Ask him to draw up a list of meals he would like to have for the week and the food items he will need to make these meals.

3.   Next, redirect his attention to the flyers and newspaper advertisements from local supermarkets. Ask him to make up shopping lists for at least two stores based on his budget, his food needs for the week, and his taste preferences.

Assessment Strategy

Review the student's shopping lists to determine whether he made the correct judgments about what brands to buy and where to buy them based on his needs and budget. Record his performance on the Diagnostic Checklist.

Follow-Up Activity or Objective

If the student achieves the lesson objective, proceed to a lesson involving the selection of a reliable person to provide a needed repair service based on the recommendations of significant others and the recommendations of agencies such as the Better Business Bureau.

SUMMARY

The ability to think critically as one interacts with oral or written communication is one of the most important skills that a student can acquire. Each day, one is bombarded with a great deal of information pertaining to all areas of one's life ranging from what to eat, wear, and drink; to where to go; what to buy; which medical procedure to choose; which investment to make; and countless other decisions. To make intelligent decisions on these and other matters, one must be able to think critically.

Advertisers and other business people are constantly telling the wise and the alert, as well as the unsophisticated and the unwary, that the products they peddle are not only good for them but are the best that can be obtained anywhere. People who are able to critically analyze and evaluate information from all types of sources, in the light of their own prior knowledge and the facts presented, will make decisions based on facts and will, therefore, make fewer bad judgments than those who do not. If students do not acquire the ability to make critical judgments on what they hear or read, they will become easy prey to false advertisements, charlatans, and other dangerous and dishonest individuals who prey on the unsuspecting and the gullible.

Educators should, therefore, prepare students to live in the real world in which the ability to think critically is not merely necessary, but absolutely crucial to survival. They must assist students in developing those critical thinking skills that will enable youngsters to protect themselves as much as possible against deceptions, and help them to make informed decisions based on careful analysis and evaluation of facts, rather than emotions and irrational thoughts.

7

PROCESSING ORAL AND WRITTEN INFORMATION FOR DECISION MAKING

The ability to communicate is not a skill confined to humans. Animals communicate with one another and, in some instances, with people. What makes human communication unique, however, is the capacity of humans to combine language and thought in expressing themselves to others and to understand what other people, who share the same linguistic system, say or write. People use language as a tool to receive and give information, to think, to manage and control their world, to interact socially with others, to define themselves, and to express feelings, desires, and hopes (Jagger & Smith-Burke, 1985). All individuals use language in this way, including those with learning and behavioral problems.

Among the most important achievements of individuals, therefore, is learning to speak their native language and becoming literate in it. These abilities enable people to relate to other people and to communicate ideas to them effectively, in speech as well as in writing. To function adequately in daily life, within all social situations, however, they must also be competent in processing oral and written information. Many cognitive operations are involved in interpreting and applying oral and written language.

Individuals with learning and emotional disabilities need special assistance in acquiring those cognitive skills essential in processing oral and written discourse. While there is no formal set of guidelines that one may use in order to communicate effectively in any situation, teachers can assist students in developing those cognitive skills that will enable them to respond appropriately to the numerous communication demands they face daily. *Among these demands is decision making.* A person's daily life is replete with decision-making situations. It is impossible to avoid making decisions, because not deciding is in itself a decision. All the decisions one makes produce results and consequences, some relatively unimportant, others extremely important. Decisions are not made in a vacuum. They are made in a context of information (Willbrand & Rieke, 1983). One's understanding of the information presented affects the type of decision one makes. It is imperative, therefore, that teachers, parents, and other caregivers help all students develop those cognitive skills necessary to process oral and written information. Acquiring these skills through meaningful experiences empowers individuals to make decisions that are appropriate and rewarding.

This chapter focuses on processing oral and written information as a foundation for making decisions based on the comprehension of the available facts. The ability to process oral and written information for the purpose of making judicious decisions involves many cognitive skills. These include:

a. Identifying symbols;
b. Discriminating among these symbols;
c. Assigning meaning to these symbols;
d. Forming concepts;
e. Seeing relationships among these concepts;
f. Activating schemata (bringing relevant previous experiences to bear on current information);
g. Making predictions;
h. Identifying main ideas and details;
i. Drawing conclusions;
j. Monitoring understandings (by asking questions of themselves);
k. Following directions;
l. Facilitating retention;
m. Identifying cues both in verbal and nonverbal communication;
n. Comprehending at the literal, interpretive, critical, and creative levels;
o. Using the facts to make meaningful choices among alternatives.

Although the basic skills for processing oral and written language are similar, there are some important differences in processing oral information.

PROCESSING ORAL LANGUAGE

A great deal of the communication that people engage in each day is done orally (Willbrand & Rieke, 1983). People talk more than they write. One talks face-to-face, over the telephone, and is exposed to oral language through listening to the broadcast media. For learning and behaviorally disabled individuals, processing this abundance of words and making sense out of this barrage can be a formidable task (Lundsteen, 1989; Norton, 1989). Following are some of the difficulties that individuals with learning problems experience in processing oral language: Inability to

1. Listen purposefully;
2. Visualize the concepts a speaker is presenting;
3. Remember or retrieve information;
4. Use previously learned ideas to understand new ones;
5. Discriminate quickly and accurately among the words and ideas of the speaker;
6. Make generalizations and draw conclusions from what is heard;
7. Translate information into appropriate action or response;
8. Be motivated due to low self-esteem.

In spite of these difficulties, it is still necessary for these individuals to receive instruction designed to assist them in oral discourse. Many students with disabilities are expected to process written discourse before they are able to process oral discourse. Students with disabilities in reading must depend heavily on the skill of processing oral information, since they cannot easily supplement oral information with written information. Teachers, parents, tutors, and other caregivers must help students to overcome these difficulties by helping them to develop the necessary cognitive skills. These skills must not be taught in isolation or as ends in themselves, rather they must be taught in the context of meaningful, decision-making experiences similar to those the individual will meet in everyday living. To make a decision based on oral information, one must first process the information. What then are the central components of processing oral language? They include: all the cognitive skills mentioned earlier plus listening, focusing, auditory discrimination of and memory for sounds and words, selecting and assigning meaning to the nonverbal aspects of the communication, combining nonverbal cues, and processing facts presented to arrive at meaning. Learning to use these skills enables individuals to make appropriate decisions based on available information.

PROCESSING WRITTEN INFORMATION

The skills necessary for processing written information have been outlined earlier. Additionally, students must visually decode words.

They must also identify in texts semantic clues such as, punctuation markers, graphic aids, and signal words. Students must understand and interpret different forms of written materials, for example: letters, invitations, bills, bank statements, labels, recipes, and notes. In one very important respect, processing written information places greater demands on the learners' competence than processing oral language. The nonverbal cues which are so very helpful in understanding and interpreting oral language are absent in written language. Therefore, apart from background experiences, comprehension of the writer's message depends solely on the ability to understand and interpret words as they appear in context.

In processing both oral and written information for the purpose of making decisions there are some specific steps that must be taken. For example:

1. Comprehending what one is expected to do;
2. Asking appropriate questions concerning purpose, alternatives, consequences, and costs in time and money;
3. Deciding on time and manner of response;
4. Deciding on whether help is needed to clarify or verify information and then locating and using these resources;
5. Deciding whether the decision can be unilateral or must be made with the input of others.

The overall purpose of this book is to assist teachers and other caregivers in helping individuals with learning problems to develop cognitive skills and utilize them in functional situations. The following section deals with using cognitive skills to process oral and written information and then applying these skills in making decisions in functional situations.

APPLYING COGNITIVE SKILLS
IN FUNCTIONAL CONTEXTS

Processing Oral Information in Face-to-Face
Contexts in Making Decisions

The following examples illustrate the cognitive stages involved in processing oral discourse in order to make decisions. The functional contexts in which the individual is operating are designated "A" and "B." "A" represents the oral discourse between the receiver and the sender, and "B" represents the results. The individual performing the decision-making function and communicating the decision after having processed the information and communicating a decision to the party(ies) concerned, is also represented under "B."

General Objective The individual will process oral information, conceptualize what is involved, then make as appropriate a decision as is possible based on his or her understanding of the facts.

Functional Context A The landlord asks an individual who has lived comfortably in an apartment for several years to move to another apartment in the same building.

Specific Objective 1 Individual understands at the literal and interpretive levels what action is expected.

Cognitive Dimensions
a. Decoding of sounds and words;
b. Assigning meaning;
c. Seeing relationships among them;
d. Activating schemata (bringing previous experience to bear on the information);
e. Conceptualizing what he or she is being asked to do;
e. Restating the proposition to him- or herself in his or her own words to check understanding;
g. Ascertaining whether or not he or she understands;
h. Asking for clarification or repetition of part or all of the message, if this is necessary;
i. Understanding the main ideas and the important details;
j. Interpreting the information by asking relevant questions. For, example, "What does this really mean?" "Why am I really being asked to move?" "What did the landlord's nonverbal behavior tell me?"

Specific Objective 2 Individual processes the information at the critical and creative levels.

Cognitive Dimensions
a. Reviews the information mentally to recheck understanding;

    b. Analyzes reasons for the request by asking pertinent questions. For example, "What will this move entail?" "How will it affect me? " "Will it cost me?" "Do I have the option to refuse to move?" "Will my decision affect others?" "If so, should they be involved in making the decision?"

    c. Decides whether there is sufficient information to make the decision independently

    d. Decides (if help is needed, what resources are available and how to utilize them)

    e. Summarizes all the facts

    f. Evaluates the situation in light of the pros and cons.

Specific Objective 3

Individual makes decision based on his or her comprehension and evaluation of the facts and communicates this to the landlord.

Functional Context B

    a. Individual decides that it is in his or her best interest to move;

    b. Tells the landlord that the decision to move has been made;

    c. Makes plans to move;

    d. Moves.

Processing Oral Information in Non-Face-to-Face Contexts in Making Decisions

General Objective

Individual will process the information, conceptualize what is involved, then make as appropriate a decision as is possible based on his or her understanding of the facts.

Functional Context A

Individual hears an announcement on the radio that water will be turned off for a certain number of hours on a specific day.

Specific Objective 1

Individual ascertains whether or not all the information has been obtained, or if it has been heard correctly. He or she decides what to do if he or she has not obtained all the correct data.

Cognitive Dimensions	a. Repeats the information to him- or herself;
	b. Decides to ensure retention by making notes;
	c. Determines that the information is important;
	d. Questions (What is it about?);
	e. Realizes that part of the information has been missed;
	f. Decides that the missing information must be obtained;
	g. Reflects (uses previous experiences to decide how to get the missing portion).

Specific Objective 2 Individual chooses one or several ways to make sure that all the relevant information has been obtained and understood.

Cognitive Dimensions	a. Reasons and asks him- or herself questions. For example, "Is this an important announcement?" "Is it for my area?" "If it is, will it be repeated?" "When?" "Will they announce it on TV also?" "On what channel?" " To what other source(s) could I turn to get the information?" "Which is the most reliable one?";
	b. Evaluates his or her sources;
	c. Chooses the most reliable.

Specific Objective 3 Individual will utilize the best source from which to obtain the information. He or she will also decide on method(s) that will be used to ensure that the information can be available for later review.

Cognitive Dimensions	a. Formulates questions to use in asking for repetition and clarification;
	b. Selects methods to ensure getting the complete message. For example, sets up a tape recorder, asks friends or neighbors to listen to the radio or the television, or to explain if they have already heard, have paper and pencil ready to write important words, phrases, and telephone numbers;

    c. Uses the source(s);
    d. Analyzes the information;
    e. Checks understanding;
    f. Seeks further explanation, if needed;
    g. Understands main idea(s) and important detail(s);
    h. Interprets the meaning;
    i. Formulates and answers questions. For example, What does this mean? How will this affect me and/or my family? What, if anything, must be done before the water is turned off? When must this be done?

Specific Objective 4　Individual having processed the information, decides the effect it will have, what has to be done, when it has to be done, and then takes suitable action.

Functional Context B　Individual, realizing that water will be needed for various purposes during the time when it will be turned off, makes necessary preparations. For example, washes clothes or takes a bath earlier than the usual time, fills up several containers of water and washes dishes. He or she also informs family members, neighbors, and friends.

PROCESSING WRITTEN INFORMATION FOR DECISION MAKING

As stated previously, processing written information involves the appliction of several cognitive skills. The individual must decode written symbols, interpret them individually, as well as a whole, then arrive at the literal, implied, critical, and creative meanings. This is a difficult task for many students including the learning disabled. Teachers, parents, and other caregivers must exercise patience in providing them with careful, effective, and practical experiences, with a great deal of positive reinforcement.

    Following are example of the steps involved in processing written information in order to make informed decisions.

General Objective　The individual will process written discourse and make as appropriate a decision

as is possible, based on his or her comprehension of the content.

Functional Context A   Individual receives a written invitation.

Specific Objective 1   Reads and tries to understand the content,
if he or she doesn't understand, he or she
decides on resources of assistance.

Cognitive Dimensions
a. Previews to get general idea;
b. Identifies source;
c. Applies word recognition skills;
d. Interprets symbols and words;
e. Asks questions to check understanding;
f. Identifies key words and phrases;
g. Organizes main ideas and important details;
h. Comprehends the literal meanings;
i. Combines background experiences with facts presented to interpret the text.

Specific Objective 2   Individual will process the information at
the critical and creative levels for the pur-
pose of making the best decision.

Cognitive Dimensions
a. Analyzes the contents by asking questions;
b. Evaluates information with reference to what acceptance will mean in terms of cost, time, and other factors;
c. Considers the relationship between him- or herself and the sender;
d. Determines the kind of party and type of dress required;
e. Determines the type of response required;
f. Prepares response. For example, constructs letter or note or selects suitable card;
g. Identifies sender's address;
h. Determines whether a gift is optional or obligatory;
i. Determines the kind of gift that would be appropriate and within his or her budget;
j. Summarizes the facts;
k. Makes decision.

Functional Context B   Individual decides to accept the invitation. He or she responds by selecting a suitable card, addresses and mails it. The individual also chooses an appropriate gift and later attends the party.

General Objective   The individual reads and understands a recipe, obtains the necessary ingredients, follows the directions, and produces the product.

Specific Objective 1   The individual will read the recipe and get the literal meaning.

Cognitive Dimensions
a. Recognizes words in the title;
b. Perceives meaning of the title;
c. Identifies key words and phrases;
d. Determines unknown word(s);
e. Selects strategies to gain meanings of unknown word(s);
f. Comprehends the sequence that must be followed to complete the recipe and arrive at the finished product;
g. Verifies general understanding.

Specific Objective 2   Individual will process the information at the critical and creative levels.

Cognitive Dimensions
a. Analyzes each part of the recipe;
b. Identifies the ingredients available and chooses which must be purchased;
c. Evaluates the ingredients with reference to health and cost;
d. Estimates amount of time and money required for the recipe;
e. Conceptualizes what the finished product will be like;
f. Summarizes what is required and what needs to be done;
g. Determines whether to use recipe or not;
h. Modifies original recipe, if necessary, to reflect health concerns, reduced cost, and number of people who will share the finished product.

Specific Objective 3   Individual decides to use the recipe, determines the ingredients needed, follows the directions, and successfully produces the end product.

Cognitive Dimensions   a. Obtains ingredients needed;
                                      b. Writes list of things that must be purchased;
                                      c. Purchases ingredients;
                                      d. Follows directions;
                                      e. Produces the product and enjoys it.

Sample Instructional Plan 1

Topic Area: Processing Oral Information for Decision Making

Designed by: Melinda Paige

Time Recommended: 1 Hour

Background Information

The student hears within the normal range; however, he experiences difficult in processing oral information to make meaningful decisions. He will need instruction in listening purposefully, developing auditory discrimination, forming concepts, understanding the main idea, and evaluating the information in order to make decisions based on his understanding of the facts.

Annual Goal (or General Objective)

The student will process oral information, comprehend it, and then make appropriate decisions based on the facts presented.

Short-Term Instructional Objective

The student processes the speaker's message and, based on his understanding of it, makes appropriate decisions.

Cognitive Dimensions

   a. Listening purposefully;
   b. Selection of most appropriate strategy to enhance memory and understanding. For example: imaging? categorizing? metacognitive? note taking?

(continued)

Sample Instructional Plan 1 *(cont.)*

  c. Eliminating distractions as much as possible;
  d. Discrimination of words and phrases;
  e. Comprehension of words, phrases, and sentences;
  f. Getting the main idea;
  g. Asking questions to verify and ensure understanding;
  h. Identifying and analyzing purpose;
  i. Evaluating pros and cons of move;
  j. Drawing conclusions;
  k. Making decision based on comprehension of information.

Functional Context

The student decides not to make a contribution to the organization and gives reasons for not doing so.

Lesson Objective

When the student is asked to make a contribution to a particular charitable organization, he listens purposefully, anticipates what is expected of him, reflects, searches for the main idea, pays attention to emotionally loaded words, analyzes nonverbal cues, establishes motive, checks comprehension, makes a judgment, summarizes, evaluates in light of previous experiences and facts presented, then makes a decision that he will not contribute. He decides on the basis of the fact that he has limited funds, and also that he needs to get more information about this particular organization from other authentic source(s). The individual communicates his decision to the speaker without offense while maintaining his position.

Materials and Equipment

  1. Filmstrips or videos of individual(s) or organization(s) asking for contributions;
  2. Sample budget;
  3. Pictures depicting various types of body language;
  4. Flash cards with various written emotionally loaded words;
  5. Pencil and paper to make a sample budget;
  6. List of names and telephone numbers of authenticating sources.

(continued)

Sample Instructional Plan 1 *(cont.)*

Motivating Activity

Discuss the purpose charitable organizations serve. Ask if the student has ever given or received any kind of assistance from any such organization. Ask if he thinks such charities actually benefit the people who really need help. Ask the student how he knew that he was giving to a worthy organization, and on what basis did he decide to make the contribution. Show the filmstrip or video of organization(s) or individual(s) soliciting.

Instructional Procedures

1. Discuss charitable giving with reference to budget considerations.
2. Show several sample budgets and involve the student in a discussion of the importance and relative unimportance of each item.
3. Discuss nonverbal cues and how they can aid in interpreting speech.
4. Show film, or allow reexamination of pictures so that the individual may identify different nonverbal cues and interpret them.
5. Allow the student to demonstrate understanding of cue(s) by acting it (them) out.
6. Juxtapose flash cards on which emotionally loaded words are written with pictures, to reinforce understanding of concepts.
7. Discuss steps one needs to follow and questions one needs to ask before making a decision to contribute to any charity.

Assessment Strategies

Determine whether the individual has:
a. Comprehended the main idea and important details;
b. Analyzed and incorporated nonverbal cues with verbal ones;
c. Identified emotionally loaded words;
d. Evaluated the information critically;
e. Asked the right questions;
f. Verified the information presented;
g. Made appropriate decisions based on all the information available.

(continued)

Sample Instructional Plan 1 *(cont.)*

Follow-Up Activity or Objective

If the individual achieves the lesson objective, proceed to a new short term instructional objective, namely, " Processing Oral Information in Non-Face-to-Face Contexts."

Sample Instructional Plan 2

Topic Area: Processing Written Information for Decision Making
Designed by: Robert Adbullah
Time Recommended: 1 Hour

Background Information

The student sees clearly and is able to discriminate among letters and words; however, she experiences difficulty in processing written information to make decisions. She will need, therefore, instruction in: interpreting words and symbols, assigning meaning to them, identifying main ideas and important details, analyzing purpose, summarizing, evaluating and using prior experiences, and comprehending the information to make appropriate decisions.

Annual Goal (or General Objective)

The student will process written information, comprehend it, and then make appropriate decisions based on the facts presented.

Short-Term Instructional Objective

The student processes the written message and based on her understanding of it makes appropriate decisions.

Cognitive Dimensions

  a. Identification of words;
  b. Interpretation of words;

(continued)

Sample Instructional Plan 2 *(cont.)*

c. Questioning to check understanding and also to clarify;
d. Selection of the most appropriate strategy to enhance memory and understanding. For example, visualizing, underlining, reading aloud, repetition, and note taking;
e. Comprehension of main ideas and important details;
f. Analyzing purpose, motive, and importance;
g. Summarizing major points;
h. Evaluating pros and cons;
i. Drawing conclusions;
j. Making decisions based on comprehension of the information.

Functional Context

The student decides to accept the invitation to a wedding and informs the sender that she will attend.

Lesson Objective

When the individual receives an invitation, she previews it, ascertains the type of invitation and the source, identifies key words and phrases, searches for the main idea, notes date and time, checks comprehension, asks herself questions to check understanding, reflects, analyzes the information, summarizes, evaluates, makes judgment in terms of relationship to the parties involved and other pertinent factors, and then decides that she will attend the wedding. She also decides on the type of gift she will take and how she will inform the sender that she plans to attend.

Materials and Equipment

1. Several samples of different kinds of invitations;
2. Samples of wedding invitations;
3. Calendar;
4. Pencil and paper;
5. Envelopes;
6. Sample budget;
7. Catalogs;
8. Samples of wedding cards;
9. Samples of gift wrapping paper.

(continued)

Sample Instructional Plan 2 *(cont.)*

Motivating Activity

Discuss different types of invitations and the kinds of responses one can or is expected to make. Discuss also the kind of gift that is appropriate. Ask the student: if she has ever received a written invitation, how she determined what kind of invitation it was, on what basis she decided to attend or not attend, what type of gift, if any, to take, and whether a gift was optional or obligatory. Then ask the student to list various kinds of invitations. Show the student different samples of invitations and encourage her to identify wedding invitations.

Instructional Procedures

1. Discuss different types of invitations.
2. Give the student four different styles of wedding invitations. Guide the student in previewing them.
3. Ask the student to identify key words and phrases.
4. Ask the student to try to identify each kind of card by simply looking at it without reading it.
5. Ask the student to identify who sent it.
6. Guide the student in reading the invitation silently and in underlining important words.
7. Encourage the student to use metacognitive strategies while reading in order to remain focused and to ensure comprehension.
8. Ask the student questions to check her understanding.
9. Ask the student to state the main idea in her own words.
10. Encourage the student to analyze the content, evaluate it, and draw conclusions.
11. Encourage the student to underline pertinent dates (of RSVP and ceremony) and time.
12. Ask the student to suggest other ways that she could use to retain the information.
13. Ask the student to identify an appropriate gift in regard to the situation and her budget.
14. Guide the student in evaluating the type of response necessary.
15. Assist the student in choosing the appropriate response.

(continued)

Sample Instructional Plan 2 (cont.)

Assessment Strategy

Determine whether the individual has:
  a. Comprehended the content of the invitation;
  b. Analyzed and evaluated it correctly;
  c. Selected the appropriate strategy for retention;
  d. Ensured retention;
  e. Combined prior knowledge with current information to make decision;
  f. Made an appropriate decision based on comprehension of the facts;
  g. Selected an appropriate gift;
  h. Made an appropriate response.

Follow-Up Activity or Objective

If the student achieves the instructional objective, proceed to a new short-term instructional objective, namely, "The individual reads and comprehends her bank statement."

Decision-Making Functional Situations

Listed below are a few examples of decision-making situations individuals encounter in their daily lives.

1. What to wear;
2. What, when, and where to eat;
3. Whom to date, court, marry;
4. Where to live;
5. What occupation to pursue;
6. What school to attend;
7. What doctor, dentist, or other health practitioner to choose;
8. Whether or not to attend a particular event or function;
9. Whether or not to follow a treatment plan;
10. Whether or not to have children;
11. Which organizations to join;
12. Whether or not to attend a particular house of worship;
13. Whether or not to purchase particular items;
14. Where should I go on vacation;
15. In what leisure-time activities should I participate?

CONCLUSION

To make these and other decisions, an individual must be able to process oral and written information effectively. This can be done only if the individual has mastered certain cognitive skills.

PART III

SOME SPECIFIC APPLICATIONS OF COGNITIVE SKILLS IN FUNCTIONAL CONTEXTS

This third section of the text applies the functional approach to cognitive development by discussing several topics that are important for students to understand and master in order to function effectively in their daily lives. The topics discussed are: (1) Time: Nature, Value, and Management; (2) Enumerating and Measuring; (3) Dependence and Independence; (4) Cooperating and Assisting Others; and (5) Identifying and Locating Materials and Resources.

Teachers and trainers may wish to apply the functional perspective to other topics that they consider appropriate to students' current status and later in their adult lives. Such topics may include: money management, choosing the right mate, planning for one's future, career changes and retraining, self-protection, and living healthily.

8

TIME: NATURE, VALUE, AND MANAGEMENT

W hat is time? It is so many seconds, minutes, hours, days, months, and years. Many definitions of time have been proffered. Each would depend on who is defining time and for what purpose. These definitions may be abstruse or quite simple. In the context of this text, however, the simple yet profound definition of Benjamin Franklin seems most applicable. He says, "Dost thou love life, then do not squander time, for *that's the stuff life is made of*" [italics supplied] (Franklin, 1961, p. 29).

Time is the most valuable, most illusive commodity and most impartial gift available to human beings. There is no other resource like it. One's life is measured in units of time. All one's acts are performed in segments of time and in relation to time. One cannot in any way evade it temporarily or escape it permanently. Solomon, the wise man, notes the manner in which one's life is inextricably bound up with time. He opines, "To everything there is a season, and a time to every purpose . . . a time to be born and a time to die . . . a time to sow and a time to reap. . . . " (Ecclesiastes 3:1-8, King James Version). Time controls one's very existence. It is indeed the *"stuff life is made of."*

Educators need to instill in the minds of students of all ages an understanding of the value of time and its relationship to the accomplishment of their present and future goals. Students must also be taught that time affects every aspect of their daily lives. For example, time is involved in meeting all kinds of deadlines and appointments, in performing various tasks, in preparing meals, and in doing business according to various specific operating schedules. One reckons with time in attending functions, using public transportation, watching different television programs, and in doing a host of other things.

One is often told to control one's time, but in the strictest sense of the word, time is uncontrollable. One cannot stop its relentless march or slow or hasten its pace. Individuals can control time only in reference to what they do with it—that is, how they use it during their existence. The success or failure of one's life is often directly related to one's concept of this important commodity and how one uses it. Coincidentally, the amount of time one has or how long one lives is not as important as the way one manages one's time. Many people live relatively short lives, yet they accomplish much, while others live very long but unproductive lives.

Time is the single most important resource available to students, how they conceptualize and use it may have far-reaching consequences for their entire lives. It is, therefore, deplorable that schools do little or nothing to inculcate in students the value of time and how to use it effectively. This subject is noticeably absent from textbooks and curricula. Even those textbooks, articles, and programs dealing with the development of effective study strategies make little or no mention of time management and its relationship to success or failure.

Educators who are charged with the responsibility of preparing students to live responsible and productive lives now and in the future should consider that teaching students the importance of managing time effectively is as crucial as teaching them to think and to become independent. Curricula at every level should include carefully planned activities to teach students how to value time, monitor it, and develop strategies for making better use of it. This is especially true today when there are so many time-saving as well as time-wasting devices available to everyone. Never in human history have there been so many gadgets, equipment, and other devices to both save and waste time. For example, electronics has brought the computer which is a great time-saving device and also television, which, although very useful in many ways, may be a very time-wasting device. Children spend hundreds of hours glued to the set at the risk of ignoring significant aspects of their lives. Students do not automatically learn to value time or become skillful in using it to achieve their goals. They need well-planned, systematic, on-going instruction on how to manage time to their advantage.

In order to manage time effectively one must first understand something about its characteristics and value. Ellis (1985) suggests some of the following important characteristics of time.

CHARACTERISTICS OF TIME

1. *Time is a unique commodity.* One cannot store it as one would store food, money, water, or wood for future use. Time does not hasten or delay at one's whim or command. It is continuously available to everyone but not indefinitely available to anyone. Its boundaries are preordained and immutable. Students need to be taught the importance of making the best use of the time they have each day, since the minutes and hours lost "today" cannot be regained, and lost time translates into loss of opportunity. Time lost cannot be regained as one may regain lost health, wealth, friendship, and love. Time cannot be hoarded, but it cannot be overspent either. One may pack more activities in a day than one normally does, but one cannot borrow some hours from tomorrow or next week and then pay it back later. Any loss of time is irretrievable.

    Many students as well as adults do not take this aspect of time into account as they function from day to day. They live as though there is an inexhaustible supply of time which they may replenish whenever they wish. To disabuse students of this misconception, teachers and trainers need to bring to learners' attention well-documented accounts and testimonies of individuals who have not accomplished all that they could have or wanted to because they misused time for many years. Students should also be provided with well-documented information on individuals who have used time effectively and have achieved their goals and objectives.

2. *Time is illusive.* It moves along imperceptibly and, therefore, is the easiest commodity to ignore because it is noiseless, tasteless, odorless, and cannot be seen or felt. This, however, does not inherently affect time. Without becoming slaves to time, students must be taught to be always aware of how they are using their time and develop strategies for making efficient use of this valuable resource. Teachers and trainers need to help students evaluate their daily activities and to ascertain what constitutes a wise use of time and what does not. Students also need assistance in understanding that being perpetually busy is not necessarily a productive use of time, nor is inactivity a waste of it.

3. *Time is equally accessible to everyone* without respect to race, color, national status, or ability. Everyone has exactly the same number of seconds, minutes, and hours in a day. Thus, time is,

perhaps, the only "equal opportunity" commodity. Some people may have more or less money or greater or lesser ability, but no one has more time than another. Some people have more things to do or do more things in a specified amount of time than others, but this does not alter the amount of seconds, minutes, and hours available in a day. Students must accept this inevitable aspect of time and utilize the time available to them with maximum effectiveness.

4. *Time is unpredictable.* Although time moves uninterruptedly, various unforeseen events may interrupt one's daily plans. These events make special demands on one's time and force one to pack more activities in an allotted time period than was anticipated. One may also have to omit activities that have been planned.

Educators should instill in the minds of students the importance of doing as much of "today's" task "today" as is possible, because one does not know unexpected circumstances that may make inroads on one's time "tomorrow."

TIME MANAGEMENT

Before students learn to manage time effectively, they must be taught how to analyze their use of time to determine when and how time is being used well or is being misused. There are several steps teachers and trainers can take in helping students to do this. First, they may ask students to monitor their time for a day and later for a whole week, by developing a time log in which learners note all their activities for that period. Before students attempt this task, however, teachers and trainers should model this assignment by presenting several examples of how *they* keep track of their time for a day or a week. They should verbalize the process they go through in determining whether time was spent wisely or not.

After students have observed demonstrations and listened to the instructor's analyses, they should be encouraged to make as honest and as detailed a list of all they do for a day or a week as is possible. Teachers and trainers should provide a format(s) that students may use to guide them as they outline all the activities of their day. Once students have completed this task, the next step is to ask them to examine their list of activities, noting the things they did that they would consider good ways of using time or bad ways of using time. Instructors should help students to understand how to evaluate "time use." Students need to learn that being busy does not mean that one is using time well, and conversely, inactivity is not necessarily a waste of time. One may waste a great deal of time doing things that are neither urgent nor important at a particular time. In evaluating effective use of time, one should always ask, "Is this the best use of my time right now?" One should also be aware that spending quiet time to think or to relax is also a judicious use of one's time.

After completing this assignment, instructors should guide students to determine how they can improve their use of time. Teachers may then evaluate these analyses to ascertain the level of the students' comprehension of effective use of time. The data obtained from this assessment may serve as a guide in planning methods and materials of instruction in time management.

EFFECTIVE TIME MANAGEMENT STRATEGIES

Before the discussion of specific strategies for managing time, it is helpful to outline the basic components of successful time management. Posner (1982) suggests five basic steps:

1. *Develop a plan* of what you intend to do during the day. This plan should also include short-term, medium, and long-term goals. Students should be encouraged to develop the habit of making and *using* daily planning guides, "to do" lists, "things-that-must-be-done-today" lists, and other guides to assist them in accounting for their time and, therefore, enable them to make maximum use of it. Educators and parents have the responsibility of directing students in setting important goals and in helping them to understand the relationship between daily use of time and the accomplishment of their goals.

2. *Construct a time log* indicating what you actually did during the day. Students may be encouraged and directed to make a list of all the activities that they were engaged in during a particular day. Teachers and trainers may assist students in doing this by helping them to log an activity right after they have done it. At the end of the day, instructors may work with students to evaluate their log to see how effectively these students have used time.

3. *Analyze* how time was well-used, how it was misused, and what were the major reasons for either. Students should be encouraged to engage in the cognitive process of analyzing what occupies their time each day. This analysis should include a categorization of activities into "important and urgent" and "unimportant and not urgent." It should also include a list of possible solutions for dealing with misuse of time.

4. *Develop solutions* for solving problems, revising and improving their plans, and creating efficient schedules.
5. *Implement the plan.* This is the most difficult step in the process, because the best formulated plans are worthless if they are not faithfully implemented. Students need guidance (through both theory and practice) in how to define and establish goals, construct daily plans, and then execute these plans.

TIME SAVERS

To determine the most effective strategies for managing time, it is necessary to examine some behaviors that may be considered time savers. Because each individual is different as are his or her goals, no one can attempt to prescribe an exhaustive list of times-saving or time-wasting activities that will accurately evaluate each person's use of time. It is also important to note that there are many cultural differences in dealing with time management. What is considered as a waste of time in one culture, may not be perceived the same way in another culture. In a general sense, however, there are many proven methods of saving time. The following are examples of some of them:

1. *Planning.* Planning takes time, but in the end, it is a very important means of saving time. Students should be taught to make a simple plan for each day or for a week. This plan should include each activity and the amount of time the individual intends to allocate to it, either as a percentage of the day or in actual number of minutes or hours. Students need to be taught not only how to plan, but the value of working with a plan. Lack of planning is probably one of the greatest causes of time waste.
2. *Setting priorities.* This is one of the best ways of saving time. Teachers and trainers should help students recognize the importance of setting priorities in reference to their goals and general activities. Students waste many hours each day doing things that are neither necessary nor important which do not relate to their short-term or immediate goals.

    Students should be instructed to write down, record on tape, or tell their goals and objectives, and then categorize these objectives in order of importance. For example, goals or daily tasks may be designated respectively as A, B, C, or D: urgent and most important, moderately important, less important, and routine. Prior to doing this assignment a student should evaluate what must be done, then prioritize each mentally. One student may rank assignments in order of due date, difficulty, amount of time required for completion, or importance of subject to his or her major or long-term goals. Another student may prioritize his or her assignments differently. The important thing is that the student understands that placing priority on what needs to be done and doing first things first, enables him or her to work more productively. Students should be encouraged to work with priority A tasks first before working on B, C, or D, because this constitutes the best use of time. If a student has more than 3 or 4 "A" priority tasks each day, he or she should be encouraged to evaluate his or her daily plan. For some students, teachers and trainers must make a special effort to help them comprehend what is meant by "priority" and why one activity or goal is more or most important than the other(s).

3. *Resist procrastination.* Procrastination is considered the great thief of time. Teachers and trainers need to assist students in establishing a happy medium between: "Never put off 'til tomorrow what can be done today" and "I can do this tomorrow, because it is not a priority for today." Students should be provided with many opportunities to analyze, discuss, brainstorm, and work with small and large groups in selecting and determining tasks that they think require immediate action and those that may be postponed until later. Teachers may assist students to construct time webs, graphs, or charts to illustrate, highlight, and clarify tasks at every level of importance.

4. *Avoid over-commitment.* Over-commitment wastes time because it encourages one to attempt more than is realistic. Thus, one is not able to give sufficient time to each task. It also encourages haste which often necessitates redoing a task. Other people's time is also wasted while the over-committed person completes "just one more task." Students must be taught to be aware of their own limitations in terms of mental capacity, health, time available, and their preference for times when they work most efficiently. (Some people work better in the morning while others work better in the afternoons or night.) Students should be guided to develop realistic insight about how much they can accomplish in light of the constraints identified above. Again, teachers and trainers should model over-committed situations and then demonstrate solutions to these problems before asking students to discuss, list, or describe ways one may become over-committed and how to avoid this problem.

5. *Learning to say "No."* This is a crucial time-saving device. One must know when to say "No" to oneself when one is tempted to either overextend oneself or to waste time. One must also

know when to say "No" to friends, relatives, and others who are habitually encroaching on one's time or who are pushing one to over-commit or enticing one to participate in activities that are neither personally beneficial nor helpful.

Here again, teachers and trainers must not assume that students can automatically develop the expertise or sophistication to determine when "No" is the most appropriate answer. They need assistance in evaluating when to say "No" and how doing so helps them to save time.

6. *Avoid over-scheduling.* Many people plan their schedules so tightly with so many activities to be accomplished in a specific timeframe that they defeat their intended purpose of saving time. They try to crowd so many activities in a specific amount of time that they often must redo things. They also fail to make adjustments for interruptions or fortuitous events. Instructors should help students to understand how to plan their activities to avoid over-commitment.

7. *Delegate or share responsibilities.* Delegating responsibilities saves time, because allowing other capable individual(s) to share responsibilities gives one more time to do other important things that one needs to do alone. Students need to know the task(s) that can be done by others who are able to do these tasks just as well or better than themselves. They also need to develop the ability to select people with whom they can work cooperatively on a task which is overwhelming and time-consuming, if attempted by only one individual. On the other hand, they must be aware of the "too many cooks spoil the broth" factor. Teachers and trainers can play an invaluable role in helping students to decide which tasks to delegate and when it is more productive to work alone or with others.

8. *Establish a "sanctuary."* It is important to establish a sanctuary to which one can escape to avoid all kinds of interruptions and to facilitate concentration and thinking. This "away-from-it-all" place may be the library, the park, a room in the house, an office—any place that will allow one time free from intrusions. Teachers and trainers may ask students to suggest places in their homes or community to which these students could retreat if they need time for quiet contemplation.

9. *Establishing a place of study.* If it is possible, students should establish a place of study and always use it for that purpose. When one sets up such a place and works there habitually for that specific purpose, one concurrently develops a mind-set for that environment. Each time a student enters, works in, or uses that particular place he or she usually assumes a posture

befitting the place and the activities that are usually performed there. For example, a library imposes on one a sense of quietude and concentration—the opposite one would experience at a party. Establishing a special place for study helps a student to focus and thus be on-task, therefore maximizing the time allotted for study.

10. *Assembling all necessary materials.* One saves time, if before one begins to work, one assembles all necessary materials to perform that task. Whether one is preparing to study, work, cook, paint, do laundry, or any other activity, it is first prudent to make an analysis of all the equipment and materials necessary to complete the task and then assemble these items in the appropriate area(s). A great deal of time is wasted when one has to stop to locate particular items that are needed when one is in the midst of doing a job. Before a student sits down to do an assignment, for example, he or she should ask, "What materials and/or equipment will I need to complete this task effectively in the shortest amount of time possible?" If a pencil is needed, it is very likely that more than one pencil is needed, or a pencil sharpener. An eraser may also be needed. If other materials such as sufficient paper, a dictionary, textbook(s), or a ruler are needed, these and all other necessary materials should be assembled in the appropriate area before one starts to work. Continuous interruptions break concentration and additional time is lost in overcoming inertia as one attempts to resume work. When one approaches one's duties in a thoughtful, well-planned manner, one saves both time and energy.

11. *Pace work periods.* Long concentrated periods of work or study are not as productive as several short well-paced periods. One gets diminishing returns from one's efforts and time when one pushes the brain to work for extended periods of time on one subject or activity without intervals of rest or change. It is better to work purposefully for short intensive periods and then rest or switch to another kind of activity. This method of work saves time because one gets more from the time one spends.

Students should be encouraged to divide their study or work sessions into several relatively short segments and use every minute of the time allotted as effectively as possible. At the end of each session, the student may rest, assemble materials for another subject or project, reward him- or herself by doing a fun activity, construct "tomorrow's to do list," or prepare part or all of a meal. The time allotted for this break, however, should be carefully observed. The student must keep his or her priorities and goals uppermost in mind and not get sidetracked by things of lesser importance.

Sample Instructional Plan

Topic Area: Time Management

Designed by: Grace Panico

Time Recommended: 45 Minutes

Background Information

The student is frequently late for school, is late with her assignments, and does not manage her time well when doing in-class assignments. For example, she does not plan ahead and obtain all needed materials before starting a project, she starts doing the assigned task immediately with no apparent plan, and she spends a lot of time looking around the room when she experiences problems with completing the task.

Annual Goal (or General Objective)

The student will identify the relationship between the effective utilization of time and the accomplishment of present and future goals, including career-oriented goals.

Short-Term Instructional Objective

The student will manage time effectively for travel within her community to recreational sites, places of business (for example, a department store), and to potential job sites.

Cognitive Dimensions

1.   Reading and interpreting bus schedules;
2.   Identifying buses and differentiating them from other vehicles;
3.   Identifying bus stops and buses by destination indicators (numbers and names);
4.   Telling time;

(continued)

Sample Instructional Plan *(cont.)*

5. Determining the amount of time needed and setting it aside in order to arrive at a bus stop on time;
6. Monitoring time during the day before the designated departure time so as not to be late to meet the bus;
7. Reading and interpreting a map of the local community and a map of the bus lines within that community;
8. Identifying time-wasters and time-savers.

Functional Context

The student will develop the knowledge and skills needed to manage time effectively in all her various activities including: self-care, household management, school-related tasks, recreational pursuits, and community-based endeavors in general.

Lesson Objective

When the student is given a local municipal bus schedule and accompanying map and asked to identify the departing and returning times of buses to at least three different locations in the community, she will identify these times and the approximate amount of time she will need to get from her home to the bus stop in time.

Materials and Equipment

1. Municipal bus schedule;
2. Map of the local community;
3. Map of the bus system;
4. Photographs of two different buses in her community and photographs of the bus stops near her home and school;
5. Watch and clock;
6. Pictures of watches from newspaper and magazine advertisements.

Motivating Activity

Show the student pictures of different watches taken from advertisements in newspapers and magazines. Discuss with her the different styles, indicating your preferences and asking her to indicate hers. Explain the importance of managing time

(continued)

Sample Instructional Plan *(cont.)*

effectively and begin a discussion on time-savers and time-wasters.

Instructional Procedures

1. Describe to the student a typical day in your life when you are not in school. Share with her how you keep track of your time on these days. Provide the student with a guide for monitoring her days and weeks. As a homework assignment, ask her to monitor her weekend time.

2. Discuss the various reasons why she might need to travel in the community: job interviews; to work; to leisure-time activities (the movies, theaters, sports stadia, bowling alleys, etc.); to make purchases of food, clothing, and furniture, etc.

3. Give her a map of the city and assist her, as needed, in locating the approximate location of her home and school. Then give her a map of the municipal bus system and ask her to locate the approximate location of her home and school and the bus lines that are near them (mark them with a marking pen). Next, show her photographs of two different buses that pass near her home and school. (Show the names appearing on the buses when they are departing and returning to her home and school.) Show her photographs of the bus stops where she is to go to catch each of the buses. Give her three different locations in her community. (As she enjoys roller skating and often goes to a downtown mall to shop, help her locate and mark these sites on the bus map. Also, assist her, if necessary, in locating and marking the company where her mother works.)

4. Review with her the bus schedule and select a time when she would like to catch each of the buses. Show her how to use the schedule to determine the time the bus departs. Give her various times of the day when she needs to be at the selected destinations. Ask her to tell you the time each bus she needs to take arrives at her bus

(continued)

Sample Instructional Plan *(cont.)*

stop so she can get to each destination on time. Once she is able to do this, proceed to the critical step of alloting enough time to get to the bus stop earlier than the designated departure time, allowing for unexpected occurrences that may delay her or for an early bus arrival.

5. Ask her to plan her entire day to avoid missing a bus either going or returning to or from a destination.

Assessment Strategy

Observe the student to see if she is able to read and interpret the bus schedule successfully and plan her time effectively for travel in the community. Record her performance on the Diagnostic Checklist.

Follow-Up Activity or Objective

If the student achieves the lesson objective, proceed to a lesson in which you assist her in using a format as a guide in managing her time.

SUMMARY

Time is the most important commodity students have. Teachers and trainers, therefore, have the critical responsibility of instructing youngsters to value it and develop the ability to use it effectively. Educators should help students to understand the relationship of their daily use of time to their goals and accomplishments and even the quality of their lives. Educators cannot and must not consider the subject of time management as merely an elective or an incidental part of the curriculum. Time is the *stuff of which life is made*; therefore, they *must* teach students how to manage it well. Neglecting to do this is a dereliction of duty. Students do not and will not automatically learn the value of time or the consequences of misusing it or how to use it productively as naturally and automatically as they learn to breathe. They must receive systematic, well-planned instruction. Their present and future success or failure is related to their conceptualization of time and how they manage it. All children need to learn how time affects their lives in negative and positive ways. Teachers and trainers are remiss if they fail to instill in them the fact that time is "indeed of the essence."

9

ENUMERATING AND MEASURING

"Measurement is the process by which numbers are assigned to properties of objects. Relationships between objects are defined by comparisons. . . . The process of measurement of any property is specific to that property, but generally either counting, reading a scale on a calibrated instrument, computation, or a combination of these are used" (Reid, 1988, p. 382). McLeod and Armstrong (1982) in their survey of teachers of students with learning disabilities in junior and senior high school programs identified measurement skills as a primary deficit area in mathematics. Mercer (1991) points out that many students with learning disabilities have problems in math that were expressed as functional and emotional problems. Problems arise in planning and monitoring time, shopping, making estimations, computing scores, interpreting recipes, and in various banking transactions. In its list of 10 basic skill areas that need to be addressed in a mathematics curriculum, the National Council of Supervisors of Mathematics (1977) includes: the application of mathematics to everyday situations and the skills of measurement.

Enumerating and measuring, using the tools of measurement, the reading and writing of measurement notations, and engaging in arithmetical computations involving various measures are fundamental aspects of math and science and of countless functional situations as basic measurement skills are applied in meaningful contexts. Reid (1988) decries the fact that elementary school teachers place undue emphasis on computation, while other aspects of math such as measurement and spatial relationships receive scant attention. In developing inquiry skills as part of science instruction, teachers and trainers must sharpen the observational skills of their students so that learners may explore subjects and events and then convert these sensory events to quantitative observations (Cain & Evans, 1984; Polloway et al., 1989).

One of the many functional situations involving enumeration and measurement is cooking. For example, individuals must count (2 eggs) and measure (1/4 cup) when cooking to ensure some degree of culinary success. One must measure and know one's various physical measurements or be measured when purchasing and seeking alterations, if one's clothing is to fit properly. Measurements are needed when purchasing curtains, drapes, bed linens, and tablecloths. Most arts and crafts projects require enumeration and measurement of some kind. Every time caregivers measure liquid medicine or count pills, they practice skills involved in enumeration and measurement. Hanging the pictures and mirrors on the walls of one's home or office requires the application of cognitions of measurement and the use of measurement tools.

To accomplish certain daily tasks, people must learn how to use the basic tools of measurement: the ruler, tape measure, and yardstick; measuring cups and spoons; thermometers, scales, watches and clocks, and other gauges. The use of measuring tools requires the reading and interpretation of numerical notations and marks appearing on such instruments and gauges. One must also engage in various arithmetical computations when dealing with measures, for example: when balancing a checkbook, when determining the time remaining to complete a task or to arrive at a destination, when modifying recipes, in sewing, and when engaging in a variety of construction activities, such as building cabinets or putting up bookshelves.

"Curriculum decisions, and the instructional strategies to accomplish them must be guided by the goal of successful adult outcomes. . . . A major emphasis of math instruction has to be functionality, leading to the acquisition of skills essential for coping with one's environment" (Polloway et al., 1989, p. 288). These authors separate functional math skills into three categories: vocational oriented-skills, everyday skills, and leisure-oriented skills. They point out that the most important source for identifying functional life skills are the students, themselves, for it is their life situations that should shape instruction.

READING MEASUREMENT NOTATIONS

Measurement notations appear on a variety of objects found in one's environment. Size labels appear on clothing shelves and racks and on the garments themselves. Quantity and ingredient specifications appear on food and nonfood containers and packages. Size specifications appear in advertisements in newspapers, magazines, and mail order catalogs. These notations must be read and interpreted carefully if one is to make judicious decisions on whether to purchase the item or not and, if so desired, to place the order with the required specificity. Recipes and written directions in and on arts and crafts kits and objects to be assembled list measures that must be read, interpreted, and implemented according to designated measurements. Prices appearing on packages and other objects, on store shelves, and in advertisements require the consumer to interpret numbers and the symbols for dollars and cents. Because of the various watch and clock faces, digital and nondigital, students must be able to read and interpret: arabic and Roman numerals (1–12 on a nondigital [analog] watch or clock), the position in space of unnumbered markings in relation to those that are marked on the face of the watch or clock, and the position in space of unnumbered markings if there are no numbered markings. Throughout one's life, one must read and interpret the various abbreviations and symbols that are used to designate measurements in both the nonmetric and the metric systems. To behave in functionally appropriate and successful ways, students must be able to:

1. Read and interpret whole numbers, fractions, and mixed numbers;
2. Read and interpret words that denote units of measurement: inches, feet, yards, and meters; ounces, pounds, and grams; teaspoons, tablespoons, cups, pints, quarts, gallons, and liters; and so forth;
3. Read and interpret abbreviations and symbols that denote units of measurement, including money;
4. Read and interpret measurement words and phrases such as: small, petite, medium, large, extra large, economy size, jumbo size, and so forth;
5. Make decisions related to the selection and purchase of food, clothing, and other items;
6. Make decisions, allocate time, and generally monitor behavior based on the "reading" of watches and clocks;
7. Make life-style, health, and safety decisions based on measurement data, for example: what to cook, what to eat (calories and fat content), what temperature to set the thermostat, whether to stop for gas, and whether to put air in a tire.

WRITING MEASUREMENT NOTATIONS

There are many occasions when it is necessary to record measurement data in writing. One needs to record one's height, age, and weight on a multitude of forms. When filling out order forms, one often needs to indicate quantity and provide size specifications. Nonverbal students and students with severe disabilities may need to write down their clothing sizes on an index card or piece of paper, because they are either unable to communicate this information orally or might not remember it when making needed purchases. Quantity and size information may need to be recorded on shopping lists, packing lists (for a vacation trip), and on inventory lists of supplies on hand in the home or on the job. In order to behave in functionally appropriate and successful ways, students must be able to:

1. Write whole numbers, fractions, and mixed numbers;
2. Write words that denote units of measurement: inches, feet, yards, and meters; ounces, pounds, and grams; teaspoons, tablespoons, cups, pints, quarts, gallons, and liters;
3. Write abbreviations and symbols that denote units of measurement, including money;
4. Write measurement words and phrases such as: small, petite, medium, large, extra large, economy size, jumbo size;
5. Enumerate and record supplies on hand to make decisions related to the selection and purchase of food, clothing, and other materials and resources.

USING THE TOOLS OF MEASUREMENT

The various types of measurement tools (size and distance, weight, volume, temperature, and time) must be demonstrated to students in functional situations. Frequent practice in using tools in these contexts must also be provided. Students must acquire the cognitive and motor skills essential for the use of the basic tools of measurement: the ruler, tape measure, and yardstick; measuring cups and spoons; thermometers, scales, watches and clocks, and other gauges. The use of measuring tools requires the following cognitive skills:

1. Differentiation of measuring instruments from all other objects;
2. Identification of which measurement instruments will be needed for a specific measuring task;
3. Differentiation between and among measuring tools that have similar function (e.g., a ruler, yardstick, and a tape measure);
4. Determination of where the needed tools are likely to be found (whether in the home or on the job or need to be purchased from a store or, perhaps, to be borrowed from a co-worker, neighbor, or classmate);
5. Location of the required tools;
6. Organization and implementation a plan of action for using these measurements, including the reading and interpreting of

the numbers and markings found on these tools and the recording of numerical data, when needed;

7. Utilization of the measurement data obtained to engage in the activity for which the measurement process was initiated.

ENGAGING IN ARITHMETICAL COMPUTATIONS INVOLVING MEASUREMENT

For a number of functional tasks, the reading, interpreting, and writing of measurement data must be accompanied by arithmetical computations. One must make various calculations when, for example: making and executing a family budget, determining the number of days left before a bill payment is overdue, estimating the number of miles left to be travelled to a destination, and calculating where to place a picture hook. In order to behave in functionally appropriate and successful ways, students must be able to:

1. Comprehend and calculate mentally or in writing using whole numbers, fractions, and mixed numbers;
2. Comprehend and meaningfully apply, mentally or in writing, symbols, words, and abbreviations that denote units of measurement: inches, feet, yards, and meters; ounces, pounds, and grams; teaspoons, tablespoons, cups, pints, quarts, gallons, and liters; etc.

Sample Instructional Plan

Topic Area: Enumerating and Measuring

Designed by: Douglas Banks

Time Recommended: 30 Minutes

Background Information

The student has had difficulty in using simple measuring tools. This interferes with the acquisition of basic functional skills involving measurement.

(continued)

Sample Instructional Plan *(cont.)*

Annual Goal (or General Objective)

The student will successfully and independently use various measuring tools, including: a ruler, scale, thermometer, and measuring cups and spoons.

Short-Term Instructional Objective

The student will use measuring cups and spoons to modify the size of a recipe.

Cognitive Dimensions

1. Reading and interpreting whole numbers, fractions, and mixed numbers;
2. Reading and interpreting words and abbreviations found in recipes;
3. Locating in the home or purchasing needed ingredients;
4. Locating in the home or purchasing needed food preparation and cooking utensils and equipment/appliances;
5. Setting burners, ovens, toaster ovens, and microwave ovens, according to required cooking temperatures;
6. Allocating the time to prepare and cook the food item(s);
7. Setting timers based on recipe requirements;
8. Comprehending and calculating mentally or in writing whole numbers, fractions, and mixed numbers to make any necessary modification(s) in recipe size;
9. Comprehending and implementing, mentally or in writing, symbols, words, and abbreviations that denote relevant units of measurement in order to make the necessary modification in recipe size.

Functional Context

The student will triple a recipe to prepare a meal to be served at a class celebration.

Lesson Objective

When the student is given a recipe for a stew and asked to triple it, he will do so correctly and then prepare and cook the item to serve to his classmates.

(continued)

Sample Instructional Plan *(cont.)*

Materials and Equipment

1. Recipe card;
2. Food preparation utensils, such as a mixing spoon;
3. Food cooking utensils, such as a spatula;
4. Pots and pans;
5. Stove;
6. Ingredients;
7. Measuring cups and spoons;
8. Serving bowl/plate and serving utensils.

Motivating Activity

Prepare a stew to be served to the student based on the recipe that will be used in the lesson. Serve it to the student and join him for lunch. (Check with his caregiver(s) first on relevant food allergies and/or likes and dislikes.) Tell the student that he will be expected to make the stew to serve at a later date to his 11 class-mates at a celebration. Tell him also that his cooked stew will be frozen and then thawed and reheated on the day of the party.

Instructional Procedures

1. Show the student the recipe card. Ask him to read the directions. Ask him how many persons the recipe will feed. Ask him to count the number of students in the class and to tell you what must be done to the recipe. Assist him in the various arithmetic computations, if needed.
2. Next, ask him to locate the ingredients and the prepara-tion utensils. Demonstrate each step in the process by ini-tiating each step and asking him to complete the process. For each measurement, model the measurement, but do not add the ingredients. Then return the ingredients to their containers, and ask him to do the actual measure-ments and add ingredients to the mixture.
3. Next ask him to review the recipe for the cooking pro-cess, locate the cooking appliances, set the temperature gauge and timer, and cook the stew.

(continued)

Sample Instructional Plan *(cont.)*

4. Assist him in carrying out the cooling and freezing processes. Assist, as necessary, and reward him for his performance and for cleaning up.

Assessment Strategy

Observe the student to see if he performed each measurement task successfully. Record his performance on the Diagnostic Checklist.

Follow-Up Activity or Objective

If the student achieves the lesson objective, proceed to a new lesson objective in which the student is expected to use a tape rule to complete a simple sewing activity.

SUMMARY

Enumerating and measuring, using the tools of measurement, the reading and writing of measurement notations, and engaging in various computations involving measures and measurement activities are essential elements in a functional education. One must enumerate and measure in the various roles one plays as one functions on a daily basis. Unfortunately, this area of mathematics instruction has been largely neglected—so many students, nondisabled as well as those with disabilities, have great difficulty in competently dealing with the multitude of measurement activities expected of independently functioning adults.

10

DEPENDENCE/
INDEPENDENCE

Self-care instruction has long been viewed as an essential part of the curriculum for many students classified as needing special education and appropriate related services. A primary goal in this instructional area continues to be the development of self-care skills that will allow students to be as *independent* of the care and attention of others, as possible, as they function in the diverse activities of daily living. Educators have long believed it is necessary for special students to develop autonomy in such daily self-care activities as: toileting, drinking and eating, dressing and undressing, and grooming. The acquisition of household management skills has also been identified as necessary for the development of personal autonomy. This additional emphasis on household management skills thus expands the goals and objectives of self-care instruction. Program goals and objectives related to *dependence* on others for assistance of various kinds rarely receive sufficient attention, although nondisabled as well as persons who are disabled will invariably require the assistance, counsel, support, and comfort of others at various times and in different situations as they strive to meet life's demands. A curriculum goal facilitating independence is obviously based on the need to minimize *overdependence* and to assist students as they are becoming more competent in independently engaging in those activities for which they possess the requisite knowledge and skills. While independence is an ideal long-range goal, individuals, whether they are disabled or not, will always be dependent on others for some functional skills and in some functional contexts. Polloway et al. (1989), in their discussion of models of transition programs, identify various life domains, including education and training for employment, community involvement, personal development, recreation and leisure, and home and family as well as *support domains* that include financial supports and emotional and physical health. Heal, Sigelman, and Switzky (1978) identify several areas that should be considered in preparing persons with retardation for adaptation to the community. These include: availability, adequacy, and access to community resources and support services and the role of benefactors, friends, and advocates. *Independence*, on the other hand, in the various roles that people fulfill as they function on a daily basis is ubiquitously identified as a principal long-range goal of special education (Drew et al., 1992; Kirk & Gallagher, 1989; Patton et al., 1990; Valletutti & Bender, 1982).

The programming emphasis on *independence* is both reasonable and logical, if for no other reason than to make the lives of caregivers less stressful. Independence is indeed a vital curriculum goal for students with disabilities, especially in preparing them for their adult years when caregivers will be more likely absent or less capable and when undue dependence on others will be less easily tolerated by society, in general. An individual's development from a dependent to an independent state for these and other reasons is seen as being a sine qua non of the maturation process. While the goal of independence is an admirable one, the reality is that, for many adults with disabilities, independent functioning is elusive and illusory. The status of adults with disabilities continues to be characterized by unemployment and underemployment, low income, lack of mobility, inadequate preparation for the various roles of adulthood (Hasazi, Johnson, Gordon, & Hull, 1989; Mithaug, Horiuchi, & Fanning, 1985; Wehman & Kregel, 1985). In commenting on adults with retardation, Fain (1986) points out that many lack a stimulating range of meaningful leisure activities and thus live lonely, inactive lives.

It has become increasingly clear that the cooperation of others and *dependence* on others for assistance, advice, and instruction is an educational goal that needs to be addressed in individualized educational and transitional plans (Wehman, Kregel, & Barcus, 1985). People must work in collaboration with others to meet both imposed and mutually agreed on goals. Collaborative efforts are necessary in the home, in the workplace, and in the community. It is important to teach students the value of cooperation, not only with their peers but also with others in the community. For example, to solve problems that affect everyone, cooperation is necessary. The resolution of problems of pollution, for instance, is dependent on well-informed and well-intentioned people working cooperatively and unrelentingly. Students, therefore, must be assisted in discriminating between those situations and conditions when independent thought and action are appropriate and when dependence on others is preferable or essential. In problem-solving situations, for example, students must determine when they can solve a problem independently, when the solution is beyond their capability, and when successful resolution will be realized more quickly with the help of others.

Teachers and trainers must assess a student's learning style with particular emphasis on *task centeredness* (Thomas & Chess, 1977). Students who are task-centered and self-confident do **not** look for clues on the quality and success of their performance in the facial expressions, the body language, the vocal inflections, and/or the comments of others. These students, because they focus on the task and disregard the reactions of people in their environment, are said to be *field independent*. *Field-dependent* students, on the other hand, **seek** the reactions of others to confirm the appropriateness, accuracy, and quality of their performance. Field dependent (or people-oriented) students, when facing situations in which group decisions are needed, will more likely recognize the need for adjustment and compromise. They will not do as well, however, when engaged in educational tasks such as arithmetical computations, if they focus on the approval or look for clues to answers from the reactions of teachers and trainers, rather than concentrating on the task at hand and arriving at the correct answer independently. In group discussion and cooperative learning tasks, teachers must assist field-independent students, on the other hand, in becoming sensitive to the feelings, needs, and values of others. When field-dependent students are able to successfully perform academically oriented skills and self-care activities, teachers and trainers during the process should avoid showing their approval or disapproval until the task has been completed. Field-dependent students who are performing successfully must be encouraged and assisted in setting their own evaluation criteria and in evaluating themselves according to these criteria, without seeking the assistance or approval of others until they have completed the task. When field-dependent students are performing independent tasks successfully and, nevertheless, persistently seek words of encouragement or approval from teachers, they must be reminded of their previous successes and firmly directed to complete the task. For example, instructors may say, "You are capable of doing that by yourself. Continue working." Students with low self-esteem and a history of failure are less likely to be task centered and are more likely to look for clues to their performance from the reactions of teachers and trainers.

IDENTIFYING DEPENDENT/INDEPENDENT SITUATIONS AND TASKS

Teachers and trainers must help students identify those situations when the youngsters can proceed without the assistance, advice, or support of others. They must also be able to identify those situations when they cannot proceed successfully unless they seek and obtain help from specific others. In order to discriminate between tasks that they can do independently and those tasks that require assistance, advice, and instruction from others, students must be able to:

1. Evaluate the task at hand (task analysis);
2. Evaluate their skills in relation to the requirements of the task and, in the absence of a specific skill, knowledge, or level of competency, make a decision as to whether or not they need assistance, advice, or instruction,
3. Determine if the requisite materials and other resources are readily available or whether they should seek assistance in locating and obtaining the items;
4. Determine whether the time available is sufficient to allow for independent task completion or whether the help of others is necessary or desirable, given time constraints;
5. Determine if they can proceed independently and, if so, set self-evaluation criteria so that the students can monitor their performance;
6. Evaluate their performance and seek help only when the process they employed does not meet established performance criteria or when the finished product is not satisfactory.

If a student's response to the six elements identified above leads to a decision that he or she requires or would benefit from the assistance, advice, and instruction of others, the youngster must be able to:

1. Identify a person who has the requisite skills and knowledge as well as the interpersonal skills to be able to provide needed assistance, advice, and instruction;
2. Ask for the assistance needed in a clear and precise manner and in a way that will likely lead to a person's willingness to assist;
3. Work cooperatively with persons providing assistance, advice, and instruction to achieve the desired goal.

FUNCTIONAL ASPECTS

There are many functional life situations in which individuals may need the assistance, advice, and instruction of others as they seek to meet the myriad demands placed on them. This is especially true during adult years when academic pressures and some intellectual demands are relaxed, following the completion of formal schooling. Despite escalating demands required of them as adults, adults with disabilities are expected to be as independent as possible. While assistance and support may not be necessary for all adults with disabilities, transitional programming from school to the life of the community must take into account their short- and long-term service needs. Expecting people with disabilities to be independent, when all people, at some time in their life, are dependent on others is a misreading of the nature of experience and, consequently, results in the misdirecting of the goals of education. Students then must be able to identify when they are dependent on others and then proceed to obtain the:

1. Assistance and cooperation of *relatives, friends, and neighbors* in times of need (when they are sick, injured, or have been physically harmed; when they need housing, food, or other necessities; when their property has been damaged, vandalized, or stolen), who will participate and share specific leisure-time experiences, and will provide advice relevant to financial, interpersonal, job-related, marital, and child-rearing problems;

2. Assistance and cooperation of *their mate* in establishing household chores and activities, including child-rearing practices, in planning and implementing a household budget, and in exploring needs and feelings, including sexual needs;

3. Assistance, *as a consumer of goods and services*, of store salespersons (in locating, purchasing, and making exchanges for needed clothing, food, appliances, and furnishings), of store managers (when problems arise, when complaints are to be registered, and when special orders are required), of physicians, dentists, and other health care providers, and of persons who provide diverse repair services:

4. Assistance, *as a traveler*, in locating places of interest for holiday travel and vacations, in locating places to which they will need to travel such as places of employment, public and private human service agencies, shopping centers, polling places;

5. Assistance, *as a learner*, from peers, teachers, and trainers in acquiring specific knowledge, information, and skills;

6. Assistance, *as a citizen*, from police, special police, security guards, fire fighters, and other community workers in times of emergency and need; of others as they participate in various community/neighborhood clean-up campaigns, recycling programs, and other conservation and beautification projects; and from social service and other governmentally sponsored and supported services and benefits;

7. Assistance, *as a worker*, in acquiring skills and pertinent information from co-workers and supervisors;
8. Assistance, *as a participant in leisure-time activities*, in acquiring specific leisure-oriented skills and in obtaining needed resources in order to participate in specific leisure-time pursuits.

Sample Instructional Plan

Topic Area: Discriminating Between Tasks That Can Be Performed Successfully and Independently and Those That Require Assistance

Designed by: Dolores Parra

Time Recommended: Two, 20-Minute Sessions

Background Information

The student has been diagnosed as having a mild-to-moderate spastic right hemiplegia. Nevertheless, she is able to perform most simple fine motor tasks involved in grooming and dressing. She needs assistance, at this time, however, in buttoning blouses and other garments with undersized buttons.

Annual Goal (or General Objective)

The student will differentiate between those motor tasks that she can perform independently and successfully and those tasks for which she must seek help. When assistance, advice, or instruction is necessary, she will seek assistance from an appropriate person in a socially acceptable manner and in a manner likely to obtain another person's cooperation.

Short-Term Instructional Objective

The student will perform most fine motor tasks involved in dressing and grooming activities, asking for help only when buttons found on blouses and other wearing apparel are too small for her to manipulate.

(continued)

Sample Instructional Plan *(cont.)*

Cognitive Dimensions

   a. Identification of garments in her personal wardrobe that she can successfully and independently button and unbutton;

   b. Discrimination of those garments in her personal wardrobe that she is unable to button independently;

   c. Selection of a female classmate who has the skill to assist her in buttoning and unbuttoning a cardigan sweater with buttons that are too small for the student to manipulate;

   d. Identification of the socially acceptable manner and the appropriate time to ask for assistance.

Functional Context

The student will seek the assistance of a peer when she has to put on a cardigan with buttons that are too small for her to manipulate in order to go out to the school yard for a recreational or fitness activity.

Lesson Objective

When the student is asked to put on something warm for an out-of-doors activity, she will select from two available cardigan sweaters—the sweater that she can button and unbutton successfully and independently. Later on in the school day, when asked to put on a cardigan with undersized buttons so she can participate in a school-sponsored charity fashion show, the student will ask a female classmate, who is physically capable of performing the task and temperamentally compatible with the student for giving assistance, for help in an acceptable manner.

Materials and Equipment

1. Cardigan with normal-size buttons;
2. Cardigan with undersized buttons;
3. An invitation to participate in a charity fashion show;
4. Volleyball.

(continued)

Sample Instructional Plan *(cont.)*

Motivating Activity

Engage the student in her preferred leisure-time activity of painting. Join her in dressing for the activity, namely putting on a protective smock requiring buttoning. Comment on the fact that she buttoned the normal size buttons on the smock without any help.

Instructional Procedures

1. Review with the students those fine motor activities that she can do independently and successfully, with particular attention to dressing and grooming tasks. Correct any misconceptions and also remind her of any specific fine motor tasks that she may have failed to mention. After this review, tell her that when she finishes painting that it will be time to play volleyball.

2. Show her two of your own cardigans, one of which has small buttons and the other has regular-size buttons. Comment that the one with smaller buttons is more difficult than the other one for you to button. Then give her two of her own cardigans, one of which has normal-size buttons and one with undersized buttons. Tell her to select the one that she can put on by herself so that she can join her classmates for a game of volleyball. Reward her for selecting the right one and for not asking for assistance in buttoning it.

3. Later in the day give her an invitation to a school-sponsored charity fashion show. Tell her that she has been asked to model the sweater that has the small buttons. Reward her if she selects a female student who has the ability and temperament to help her and asks for assistance in a way that will likely get the selected peer to cooperate. Reward and provide language models as needed.

Assessment Strategy

Observe the student to see if she asked for help when needed from an appropriate female peer and did so in a socially acceptable manner. Record your observations on the Diagnostic Checklist.

(continued)

Sample Instructional Plan *(cont.)*

Follow-Up Activity or Objective

If the student achieves the instructional objective, proceed to a lesson objective that stimulates the student to ask for instructional help from a peer when confronted with a vocationally oriented assembly task.

SUMMARY

While the development of independence in students (especially those students with disabilities who are likely to be more dependent on others) is a principal educational goal, teachers must also provide students with learning experiences that help students determine when they should depend on the assistance and cooperation of others. Students with disabilities must be helped to identify when they can perform successfully and independently, when they have to depend on others (because of the nature of the task or because of the nature of their disability), and when they should seek the assistance and cooperation of others to expedite performance and/or improve the quality of the eventual product. Parents and teachers of children with disabilities must be helped to differentiate between those situations and tasks in which help is needed and those situations and tasks in which (no matter how much easier and quicker it is for them to do it for the child) the child should be expected to perform the task independently and successfully with minimum support and reinforcement.

11

COOPERATING WITH AND ASSISTING OTHERS

Typically, instructional programs for students with disabilities concentrate on those skills essential to their role as learners—learning from teachers, parents, siblings, and significant other caregivers or trainers. The functional approach to instruction, however, which seeks to prepare students for their future role as productive and successful adults must be concerned with developing those skills needed by adults in their role as assistant, advisor, and instructor.

It is understandable that educators will often overlook this functional area, especially when one is teaching young students because they still have so much to learn. It is also to be expected that teachers will frequently ignore identifying program goals and objectives for this instructional area when teaching students with disabilities. This is likely because these students, typically, have been viewed as being the recipients, *not* the providers, of assistance, advice, or instruction. If teachers and trainers ignore this facet of the curriculum, however, they fail to prepare students for those occasions during the school years and later in adult life when they will be called upon to cooperate with others. To work cooperatively with others, students will need to be able to:

1. develop the self-confidence necessary to function as a provider of assistance, advice, or instruction;
2. identify when a classmate, someone in their family, a friend, or co-worker is requesting or is in need of assistance, advice, or instruction;
3. analyze the nature, scope, and sequence of an instructional task;

4. synthesize and execute the plan in a training or tutoring situation;
5. stimulate interest and involvement;
6. create or prepare creative activities for instruction;
7. evaluate the outcome of the assistance or instruction.

There are several means available to teachers and trainers through which they can assist students in learning to cooperate with and assist others. Some of them are peer tutoring, the buddy system, and cooperative learning. Teachers and trainers should understand how each of these systems can enable students to develop the ability to cooperate and work well with others. Instructors should not haphazardly divide students into peer groups and buddy systems unless they understand which children can work well together, which students have specific abilities necessary to work well with others, which students need peer tutoring and for how long, and which students have the skills and abilities necessary to function as a tutor or buddy.

PEER TUTORING

One of the most valuable instructional strategies available to teachers and trainers is peer tutoring (Bender & Valletutti, 1985; Cooper & Cooper, 1984; Lloyd, Crowley, Kohler, & Strain 1988). Research studies demonstrate that peer tutoring is an effective instructional strategy for students with learning and behavioral disabilities in the elementary and secondary grades whether these students are tutees or tutors (Eiserman, 1988; Scruggs & Richter, 1986). Academic progress and more positive attitudes about learning, academic content, and students with disabilities frequently are realized when this student-directed instructional strategy is employed (Eiserman, 1988; Schuler, Ogulthorpe, & Eiserman, 1986; Scruggs, Mastropieri, Veit, & Ogulthorpe, 1986). Cooper and Cooper (1984) have described four prototype peer-learning forms: *parallel/coordinate* in which two or more children working on their own projects are encouraged to exchange comments; *didactic* in which one acts as a teacher; *collaborative* in which the students alternate the teaching role; and *onlooker* in which one student looks at what another student has done. The *didactic* and *collaborative* peer learning discourse forms have come to be known as peer tutoring. A peer-tutoring approach requires teachers to: identify instructional objectives; to identify, for each student in the class or in a group, areas of the curriculum for which he or she can serve as a tutor of classmates; match students; prepare materials; select sites and establish schedules; plan formats; train tutors; monitor progress; evaluate the tutoring sessions; and communicate results (Olson & Platt, 1992). Furthermore, prospective tutees for each selected tutor must also be identified and matched according to needed skills and personal and temperamental compatibility. A caveat must be observed however. Students with disabilities are invariably placed in the tutee role. Every student, whenever possible, however, must serve in both roles: tutor as well as tutee. Students with disabilities who are always placed in the role of tutee are likely to become increasingly resentful and hostile to both teachers and peers as further damage may be done to their already diminished self-esteem. These students too need to experience and acquire those skills needed to function as tutor if and when the necessity arises.

It may be difficult, however, for a teacher to find curriculum areas for which the less able students in the class (whether they have been identified as special or not) can serve as tutors. Teachers and trainers, nevertheless, must take the time and effort to do so. Once prospective tutor-tutee pairs or teams have been identified, teachers must then proceed to assist the designated tutors in acquiring those instructional (including reinforcement and practice) skills necessary to assist their tutees in acquiring an identified instructional objective(s). In effect, peer tutors become "student teachers" who, under the teacher's guidance, teach planned lessons to their assigned peer(s). Peer tutors must be assisted in: obtaining and using instructional materials, providing verbal and other prompts, applying remedial techniques, and rewarding progress with the teacher acting as "consultant" or "troubleshooter" during the actual peer-tutoring sessions (Craig, 1983). Tutees must also be prepared for their role. Both tutors and tutees must be rewarded for "good teaching" on one hand and for "good learning" on the other hand.

BUDDY SYSTEMS

A second instructional strategy that has been successful in teaching nondisabled and students with disabilities has been the buddy system (Valletutti & Bender, 1985). The buddy system allows for the continuation of tutor-tutee relationships outside the classroom. It encourages and supports the development and maintenance of friendships (a major goal or unit of study in a functional curriculum) as students advise and counsel each other, participate together in community-based learning activities, collaborate in cooperative learning assignments, study together, and, ideally, participate in productive and enriching leisure-time experiences. In order for the buddy system to work outside the classroom, parents must be contacted, the procedure explained, and the parents' cooperation assured before proceeding. Parental attitude is crucial to the success of this approach, because parents may possibly view this approach as an invasion of their privacy, a burden, or as an unwarranted intrusion into their family life.

COOPERATIVE LEARNING

Another student-directed instructional strategy is cooperative learning. In its usual format, cooperative learning groups work together as teams of three or four members. Like peer tutoring, cooperative learning strategies increase academic achievement and facilitate positive attitudes toward both content and classmates (Johnson, Johnson, & Maruyama, 1983). Rejection of mainstreamed students with disabilities appears to decrease in cooperative learning situations (Slavin, Leavey, & Madden, 1984). According to Olson and Platt (1992), "There are essentially four models of cooperative learning: a). the jigsaw approach, b). the group project, c). the competitive team approach, and d). Team-Accelerated Instruction" (p. 300). In the jigsaw format, each member becomes an expert in an aspect of the material or task. In the group project format, students are expected to pool their knowledge and skills to complete an assigned task, solve a problem, or create a product. In the competitive teams format, students are introduced to new information, then study together, and, finally, take quizzes or participate in tournaments as teams. Finally, in the Team-Accelerated Instruction format, individualized instruction is combined with cooperative learning. Students, based on their demonstrated competencies, are assigned different levels of a group task and are expected to bring newly emerging skills to the group effort (Slavin, 1988).

Valletutti and Christoplos (1990) have developed additional game formats applicable to academic learning. These Cooperative Academic Games (CAGs) are teacher-made card games that actively involve children in learning all academic subjects and in acquiring informal social and interpersonal skills. CAGs provide teachers with an efficient and motivating way to develop their students' knowledge and skills as well as their social, interpersonal, and thinking skills. These games involve continuous and positive participation by all students in a class or group. Such active, continuous participation maximizes attention and motivation. When all students are striving for an overriding group goal (as required by CAGs), each student's contribution is needed and, therefore, welcomed by all in the group. There are no winners or losers. High and low achievers participate at their own level. Neither individuals nor groups are hampered by the limitations or inadequacies of any one student. Often in activities identified as being cooperative and therefore not potentially damaging to the self-esteem of less competent members of the class, team members feel penalized by having a less competent member participate. In CAGs such resentment is precluded by the nature of the CAG formats.

CAGs are useful as an effective and efficient classroom drill. Each CAG is replayed four or five times. With each successive replay, the group attempts to reduce the time needed to complete the CAG. With each replay, students are given or expected to take a different card in the game, thus broadening the drill experience, making it both more efficient and effective. CAGs provide teachers with a highly efficient and effective strategy for acquiring and practicing the rote skills subsumed under the traditional academic subjects. CAGs, by their cooperative nature, foster critical social, interpersonal, and cognitive skills. Cooperation is one of the social skills most needed to solve the problems arising in the world and workplace and prevent and diminish problems of disruption and isolation among children.

FUNCTIONAL ASPECTS

The role as assistant, advisor, tutor, or teacher is manifested in a variety of functional situations, capacities, and roles in which the student assists others in acquiring teacher and trainer identified knowledge, skills, attitudes, and values.

1. *As a learner*, the individual must be able to: assist classmates in following an activity schedule, perform specific assigned tasks, assist classmates during fire drills and real emergency situations, and engage in diverse cooperative and collaborative efforts and projects.
2. *As a parent*, the individual must be able to: teach his or her children to feed themselves, undress and dress themselves, be independent in toileting, brush their teeth, wash and bathe themselves, prepare meals, behave in healthy and safe ways, perform simple household tasks, care for younger siblings and for older family members, set daily goals and objectives, establish and maintain good interpersonal relations, acquire preacademic and academic skills, develop fine and gross motor skills

and a healthy body, deal with their sexuality, behave in healthy and safe ways, travel in the community, engage in leisure-time and recreational activities, and acquire essential vocational skills.

3. *As a family member and friend*, the individual must be able to: assist relatives and friends in their time of need, share recipes and teach relatives and friends how to prepare meals, demonstrate how to carry out household tasks, provide advice when requested, assist relatives and friends in making financial decisions, and demonstrate how to engage in diverse leisure-time and recreational activities.

4. *As a member of a household unit*, the individual must be able to: demonstrate specific household tasks and respond appropriately to members of their household unit who request or need help.

5. *As a worker*, the individual must be able to: demonstrate how to behave appropriately according to specified work rules and policies, and carry out specific work-related skills and tasks.

6. *As a participant in leisure-time activities*, the individual must be able to demonstrate how to: play a variety of games, engage in various sports and physical fitness activities, participate in outdoor activities, engage in nature study, pursue diverse hobbies, engage in arts and crafts activities, and participate as an observer or performer in various entertainment activities.

Sample Instructional Plan

Topic Area: Preparing Students To Play the Part of a Teacher

Designed by: Dorothy Waage

Time Recommended: Two, 30-Minute Periods

Background Information

The student has been experiencing difficulty in playing the role of tutor in various peer-tutoring activities.

Annual Goal (or General Objective)

The student will teach someone how to perform a simple task.

(continued)

Sample Instructional Plan *(cont.)*

Short-Term Instructional Objective

The student will teach someone how to perform simple household tasks, including cleaning and simple household repairs.

Cognitive Dimensions

1. Development of the self-confidence necessary to function as a "teacher";
2. Identification of when a classmate is seeking help;
3. Analysis of the nature, scope, and sequence of an instructional task;
4. Synthesis and subsequent execution of a teaching plan;
5. Ability to stimulate interest and involvement;
6. Evaluation of outcome of the instructional activity.

Functional Context

The student will assist a classmate who seeks his help to change the burned-out light bulb on a table lamp and to clean up broken glass.

Lesson Objective

When the student is asked by a classmate for help in changing a light bulb and the classmate begins to clean up broken glass in an unsafe way, the student will teach his peer to: change the light bulb safely and to safely clean up broken glass.

Materials and Equipment

1. 2 plates, 2 dessert dishes, 2 spoons, 2 table knives, 2 glasses, and 2 napkins;
2. Fruit juice, a jar of peanut butter, and 2 bananas;
3. Loaf of bread and crinkled up clear paper from several loaves of bread to simulate broken glass;
4. Quart of low-fat frozen yogurt;
5. Burned-out 60 watt light bulb;
6. New 60 watt light bulb;
7. End table and table lamp;
8. Brush, dustpan, and metal wastebasket;
9. Work gloves.

(continued)

Sample Instructional Plan *(cont.)*

Motivating Activity

Tell the student that he will invite one of his peers for lunch. (Specify the student peer since this peer must be able to carry out the role play.) Tell him that the menu will be peanut butter and banana sandwiches, orange (or other fruit) juice, and frozen yogurt for dessert.

Instructional Procedures

1. Review a previous lesson in which the student was taught how to replace a burned-out light bulb and then reverse roles and allow the student to replace one. Also, review the safe way to clean up broken glass with a brush and dustpan, while wearing work gloves. Practice with the student acting as teacher, demonstrating for teacher and peer how to clean up broken glass safely. (Use clear paper, like that found on the inside of a package of bread that you have crinkled up to simulate glass.)
2. After preparing the student peer for the role play that will begin in the middle of the second part of this lesson, assist the student in setting the table and preparing the lunch. (Set the table in a somewhat dark area of the classroom and place an end table and lamp next to it. **Do not**, however, turn on the lamp. It has a burned-out bulb in it!)
3. Demonstrate how to invite a friend for lunch. Ask the student to model you. Once he has successfully done so, ask him to invite his friend.
4. During the lunch, the peer will be asked to turn on the light. The teacher may say, "The bulb must be burned out. Do you have a new one? I need your help because I never changed a light bulb before!" Ask the student to teach his classmate how to change the light bulb. Reward him for doing so clearly and successfully.
5. Sometime later, the classmate will knock the burned-out bulb off the table. Ask the student to teach his classmate how to clean up the broken glass safely and successfully. Reward him for doing so clearly and safely.

(continued)

Sample Instructional Plan *(cont.)*

Assessment Strategy

Observe the student to determine whether he has taught the two skills successfully. Record his performance on the Diagnostic Checklist.

Follow-Up Activity or Objective

If the student achieves the instructional objective, proceed to a lesson objective in which the student is expected to teach a child how to wash and dry toy and then real dishes.

SUMMARY

This chapter emphasized the development of the knowledge, skills, and attitude/values needed to work cooperatively with others as an assistant, advisor, and tutor. A number of essential component skills have been identified, including: the development of the self-confidence necessary to function as a tutor; the identification of situations in which a classmate, someone in their family, a friend, or co-worker is requesting or is in need of assistance, advice, or instruction; the analysis of the nature, scope, and sequence of an instructional task; the development and implementation of a cooperative plan of action; and the ability to stimulate interest and involvement. Several strategies available to teachers and trainers relevant to the development of this competency have been explored: peer tutoring, the buddy system, and cooperative learning. In addition, various functional skills relevant to the tutoring and assisting role are enumerated for the following social roles that students fulfill: as a learner; as a parent; as a member of a family unit, friend, and neighbor; as a member of a household; as a worker; and as a participant in leisure-time activities.

12

IDENTIFYING AND LOCATING MATERIALS AND RESOURCES

As humans function on a daily basis in the various roles they play in meeting the societal demands made on them, they must perform a variety of motor tasks. Fine motor tasks for young students include: leisure-related activities such as painting, playing with puzzles, and cutting and pasting as well as self-care activities such as tieing shoelaces, fastening and unfastening buttons, and zipping zippers on clothing and book bags and toiletry cases (Bender & Valletutti, 1985). Fine motor tasks for older students include: a wide range of arts and crafts activities such as paper crafts, pottery or clay sculpturing, jewelry making, woodworking, leather craft, and weaving (Polloway et al., 1989). Whenever one is confronted with a motor task that requires the use of tools, equipment, and other resources, one must be able to: identify which materials and resources are needed; differentiate between and among those that are similar in shape, size, color, and function; determine where they are likely to be located (whether on hand or to be purchased); locate them; organize the process; and then engage in the desired activity. In this context, the term equipment is used to refer to machines and other large apparatuses, which are really oversized tools. Refrigerators, vending machines, automobiles, and elevators are examples of such equipment.

When one wants to brush one's teeth, one must identify his or her toothbrush, differentiating it from all other available brushes and from the toothbrushes of other people in the home. This identification may involve differentiating between and among colors, sizes, and shapes. Individuals, first of all, must be able to differentiate between things that are brushes and all other objects. An individual then must be able to differentiate toothbrushes from other brushes. There are many different brushes that one might find in the home: toothbrushes, hairbrushes, nail brushes, and scrub brushes. Students must then be able to decide which brush is the appropriate one needed to perform the desired task. Subsequently, one must determine where this essential tool is likely to be located and then differentiate his or her toothbrush from all other toothbrushes in the bathroom. Whenever his or her toothbrush needs to be replaced and there is a replacement in the home, the individual, subsequently, must be able to find the new toothbrush in its likely storage area. The individual must also be able to engage in similar mental processes in order to obtain other needed materials necessary for brushing his or her teeth. The person must also be able to identify the water faucets and temper the water appropriately.

IDENTIFYING NEEDED MATERIALS AND RESOURCES

In assisting students to identify resources that they need to function in their daily lives, teachers and trainers must help them conceptualize that various parts of their bodies are vital resources that may function as instruments to perform various tasks. It is the students' brains that generate the ideas that lead to acts that they want to perform (Siegler, 1983). The brain operates as the great generator of thought which initiates the actions the body then performs; for example, the eyes, mouth, the hands, and the feet execute the functions directed by the brain. Teachers and trainers need to help students understand this concept as youngsters identify resources they use in their daily lives.

Students need to be taught how to use their body as their basic resource. They need to understand and then discover the capabilities of various parts of their body through various work-oriented activities (sharpening a pencil, sewing a button on a shirt or blouse, and lifting a heavy package) and diverse recreation activities (dancing, cutting paper and cloth for a collage, playing games, and engaging in physical exercise) (Smoot, 1985). They also need to understand that the brain and various parts of the body operate interdependently to perform different tasks in conjunction with external resources. Sometimes the whole body is used to perform a task; other times only parts of the body are used—for instance, the arms, hands, and shoulders. In effect, one's body parts are tools that help to accomplish various functional tasks in the home, school, and community.

Additionally, students should be taught that people have created tools and equipment to help accomplish life's many tasks more easily and successfully. Tools are needed to simplify a task, to augment the power produced by movements of the body and its parts, and to facilitate successful performance.

The home setting provides an excellent site for discovering, manipulating, and exploring the tools that have been developed to simplify work and conserve time and energy. The kitchen has many tools used for preparing and consuming food. To help students gain a clear firsthand understanding of equipment and tools, teachers and trainers should take them to observe demonstrations and provide youngsters with opportunities to view and use interactive tools typically found in a home. It is very important for teachers and trainers to provide students with the opportunity to handle, identify, manipulate, and use these tools. Each tool first should be explained by the teacher and then the students given a chance to examine and then describe each tool's various functions. During the tour, teachers and trainers may demonstrate the use of a tool in the following manner: (1) Announce that it is snack time and give each student a walnut. (2) Ask everyone to use their hands to break the shell so they can get the kernel. (3) When youngsters discover that they are unable to do so, show them a nutcracker and say, "Do you know what this is? Have you ever seen it before? What do you think it is used for?" If they know the name, ask them to tell everything they know about the nutcracker. If the students cannot identify the tool, ask them to guess its use. If they cannot guess, say to a student, "Take it and look at this interesting tool. I am also hungry, and there is something good to eat, but we are unable to eat it because we cannot break the shell." Then say, "My hands aren't strong enough tools to do this job. How do you think I could use this instrument to break this shell? What part of this instrument do you think could be used to break this shell?" Then proceed to crack the shell, showing them how the nutcracker works. (4) Ask the students to describe what happened and why they think the tool is called a nutcracker. Utilizing a problem-solving and functional approach, the teacher may use the same procedure with other tools and equipment found in a home environment. Finally, trips should be arranged to various locations in the community where tools are available for purchasing, for example, department stores, hardware stores, and discount stores and have students identify the tools found there.

Throughout these activities, care must be taken to assist the student in making verbal associations between each tool and its function(s). That is, "A *nutcracker* is a tool that helps us to *crack nuts.*" "A *dishwasher* is a piece of equipment that helps us to *wash dishes.*" "*Scissors* help us to *cut* paper and cloth!" "A *fork* helps us to *pick up things.*"

DIFFERENTIATING AMONG MATERIALS AND RESOURCES

The shape of an object is the principal attribute by which one can differentiate one item from another. Instructional activities, therefore, should be developed which demonstrate and emphasize the relationship between the shape of an object or tool and its function. For example, while showing the student a pair of scissors one may ask students why they think scissors are shaped the way they are. If they fail to do so, teachers may give them the relevant explanation. This approach should be repeated with many other tools, to help the student understand the relationship between function and form. For example, ask the students to explain why a pencil or a screw driver has its particular shape. Give students sufficient time to explain.

Another method of identifying tools is by size. Students must be asked to explain why a little paint brush used for detail work is smaller than one used to cover large areas with paint. A snow shovel is larger than a toy shovel. A tablespoon is larger than a teaspoon. A baby's crib is smaller than a queen-size bed, and a passenger jet plane is larger than a helicopter. In these examples, students must first demonstrate the appropriate use of each item and then demonstrate their understanding of the function of each object by describing it orally. For example, in commenting on their demonstration of the use of a snow shovel and a shovel that is part of a toy pail and shovel set, teachers or trainers may first ask the students to explain that, although the items are different in size, each is called a shovel. If they are able to do so, teachers and trainers may proceed by asking, "Why do you think they are both called shovels?" Then ask the students to explain in their own words how each type of shovel differs in size and function. Teachers and trainers should evaluate the responses of their students to ascertain whether or not youngsters fully understand the critical features that differentiate the items. The instructor may continue by placing the shovels at different locations in the classroom and creating several problem-solving situations to reinforce the correct use of the different types of shovels. For example, teachers and trainers may present various functional situations: Ask students how they might help a friend who lent them a snow shovel during the winter by asking them to show you the shovel they would lend a friend going to the beach on vacation. Ask the student to tell which shovel would be used to help a grandparent to clear a walkway after a snowstorm.

A third way of identifying needed resources is by color. As was discussed earlier in the example of the toothbrush, an individual may need to distinguish among his or her toothbrush and the ones that belong to other members of the household by using color clues. Teaching students to use color as a critical distinguishing characteristic may be accomplished by involving youngsters in activities that require the identification of personal objects by color. For example, they might identify such personal belongings as clothing, toys, and books.

IDENTIFYING AND LOCATING
NEEDED MATERIALS AND RESOURCES

Students should be helped to understand the relationship that exists between an object's function and the place where it is usually stored. For example, spoons, forks, and knives are used for eating; therefore, they are likely to be found in the kitchen. As these utensils are used for cooking and eating, they should be kept clean and, therefore, are likely to be located in a kitchen drawer. Toothbrushes and toothpaste would be located in the bathroom, as that is where people usually brush their teeth. Household tools are found in a toolbox that may be kept in the basement, garage, or closet. Refrigerators and stoves are kept in the kitchen.

A suitable teaching activity might involve teachers and trainers in several different role-play activities in which they model the thought processes that one engages in when one is determining where to go: when seeking a light bulb to replace a burned-out one, when looking for a screwdriver to do a simple repair, and when replacing toilet paper when a roll is empty. After engaging in several similar role-playing activities, teachers and trainers should give the students similar problems to solve, and encourage them to verbalize their thought processes. For example, ask the students to explain where they would locate the materials to make sandwiches for themselves and some friends as they share a recreational activity.

Another aspect involved in locating needed materials and resources is knowing where to find items if not available at home. Items may need to be purchased because they have been depleted, are no longer functional, or have not been needed in the past. If these items are to be obtained from a place unfamiliar to the student, teachers and trainers need to provide youngsters with relevant information necessary to help them determine how to locate the resources they need in a particular environment. For example, it may be difficult to locate certain items in some stores today, as many stores now carry a wide variety of merchandise, organized in ways that may be confusing to the average consumer. In spite of this, students should be provided with frames of reference and strategies to assist them in problem solving.

Instructional activities should be implemented that assist students in identifying a clothing store as the place one might find various articles of clothing, a jewelry store as a place where one is likely to find jewelry, and a paint store as a place where one will be able to locate paint and paint brushes for sale. In dealing with department stores, students can be helped by asking them to identify the section or counter where one might go to find: women's shoes, men's clothing, housewares, and electronic equipment.

Sample Instructional Plan

Topic Area: Identifying Needed Materials and Resources

Designed by: Elaine Karpf

Time Recommended: 30 Minutes

Background Information

The student has had difficulty in identifying and locating simple tools needed to perform self-care and simple household tasks.

Annual Goal (or General Objective)

The student will identify, locate, and then use tools found in the home to perform self-care and simple household tasks.

Short-Term Instructional Objective

The student will identify, locate, and use his or her toothbrush.

Cognitive Dimensions

1. Understanding that a toothbrush is needed in order to brush one's teeth;
2. Differentiation between and among other tools (brushes) that are similar in shape, size, color, and function;
3. Determination as to where toothbrushes are likely to be found (whether available or to be purchased);
4. Identification of one's own toothbrush, discriminating it from other toothbrushes found at the same location.

(continued)

Sample Instructional Plan (cont.)

Functional Context

The student will brush his or her teeth after lunch.

Lesson Objective

When the student is asked to brush his or her teeth after lunch, the child will locate his or her own toothbrush, differentiating it from the toothbrushes of classmates, and then brush his or her teeth.

Materials and Equipment

1. Toothbrush holder;
2. 6 paper cups;
3. 6 small toothpaste tubes;
4. A hairbrush, nail brush, and two thin paintbrushes;
5. 2 unpainted pictures;
6. Paint set;
7. Paper towels;
8. 6 bars of soap;
9. 6 different color toothbrushes—blue (the student's), red, yellow, green, purple, and orange.

Motivating Activity

Tell the student that he or she has several household and personal chores to do and needs certain tools. Ask the student to decide which tool to use for each task. Ask the younster to look at his or her hands to see if they are dirty, and ask the student to suggest the materials that would be necessary for cleaning his or her hands. Then ask the student to choose the right tool for the job from a selection of materials. Then provide the student with a group of materials and ask him or her to select the correct tool for brushing the hair. Next give the student a picture of an object with which the child is familiar and a paint set with various colors. Ask the student to select the appropriate colors to paint that object.

Instructional Procedures

1. Tell the student that there will be a special lunch today with invited guests (the students from a nearby classroom).

(continued)

Sample Instructional Plan *(cont.)*

Remind all of the students to remember to wash their face and hands before lunch and then brush their teeth after they have eaten. Assist them if needed in washing and drying their face and hands.

2. After lunch, review with them the brushes used in the motivating activity. Add his or her toothbrush (blue) to the other brushes. Then ask him or her to point to the brush he or she would use to perform different household and personal chores. Reward as necessary.

3. Next place the six different toothbrushes (blue, red, yellow, green, purple, and orange) out on paper towels. Point to each brush and say, "Do you know whose toothbrush this is?" Repeat this activity for each toothbrush, ending with the student's toothbrush. Rearrange the toothbrushes, asking him or her to point to his or her toothbrush. Rearrange to give each student a chance to respond.

Assessment Strategy

Observe the student to see if the child has selected his or her own toothbrush. Record the performance on the Diagnostic Checklist.

Follow-Up Activity or Objective

If the student achieves the instructional objective, proceed to a lesson objective in which the student is expected to identify and locate the tools needed to prepare a simple meal.

SUMMARY

This chapter has reviewed the processes involved in identifying and locating needed materials and resources. A number of essential processes are involved: identifying what resources are needed; differentiating between and among various resources by shape, size, color, and function; determining where items are likely to be located; locating and identifying these needed materials; and organizing and engaging in the motor process. All students, including those with learning and behavioral disabilities, must develop the ability to identify and locate various tools and equipment necessary for the successful and facile performance of various functions that are part of their daily experience.

REFERENCES

Adams, M., & Bertram, B. (1980). *Background knowledge and reading comprehension.* (*Reading Education Report No. 13*). Urbana, IL: University of Illinois (ERIC Document Reproduction Service No. ED 181 431).

Adams, M., & Collins, A. (1986). A schema-theoretic view of reading. In H. Singer & R. Ruddell (Eds.),*Theoretical models and processes of reading* (pp. 404-425). Newark, DE: International Reading Association.

Alexander, J.E., Davis, A.R., Heathington, B.S., Huff, P.E., Knight, L.N., Turner, T.N., & Wynn, S.J. (1983). *Teaching reading* (2nd ed.). Boston: Little, Brown.

Ames, C., & Ames, R. (1984). Goal structures and motivation. *The Elementary School Journal, 81,* 87-96.

Anderson, R., & Pearson, P.D. (1984). A schema-theoretic view of basic processes in reading comprehension. In P.D. Pearson (Ed.), *Handbook of reading research* (pp. 241-255). New York: Longman.

Arendt, H. (1977). Thinking II: *The New Yorker,* (November): *28,* 114-163.

Austin, M., & Morrison, C. (1963). *The first R: The Harvard report on reading in elementary schools.* New York: Macmillan.

Bachor, D. (1979). Using work samples as diagnostic information. *Learning Disability Quarterly, 2,* 45-52.

Bagnato, S. (1980). The efficacy of diagnostic reports as individualized guides to prescriptive goal planning. *Exceptional Children, 46,* 554-557.

Baker, L., & Brown, A. (1984). Metacognitive skills and reading In P.D. Pearson (Ed.), *Handbook of reading research* (pp. 353-394). New York: Longman.

Bender, M., & Valletutti, P.J. (1982). *Teaching functional academics to adolescents and adults with learning problems.* Baltimore: University Park Press.

Bender, M., & Valletutti, P.J. (1985). *Teaching the moderately and severely handicapped: Curriculum objectives, strategies, and activities: Vol 1. Self-care, motor skills and household management.* Austin, TX: PRO-ED.

Bersoff, D. (1973). Silk purses into sow's ears: The decline of psychological testing and a suggestion for its redemption. *American Psychologist, 10,* 892-899.

Beyer, B.K. (1983). Common sense about teaching thinking skills. *Educational Leadership, 41,* 44-49.

Beyer, B.K. (1984). Improving thinking skills—Defining the problem. *Phi Delta Kappan, 65,* 487.

Billings, N. (1929). *Determination of generalizations basic to social studies.* Baltimore: Wardwick and York.

Bloom, B.S. (1956). *Taxonomy of educational objectives. Handbook 1: Cognitive domain.* New York: Donald McKay.

Brolin, D.E. (1986). *Life-centered career education: A competency-based approach* (rev. ed.). Reston, VA: Council for Exceptional Children.

Browder, D.M., & Snell, M.E. (1987). Functional academics. In M.E. Snell (Ed.), *Systematic instruction of persons with severe handicaps* (pp. 436-468). Columbus, OH: Merrill.

Brown, L.F., Branston, M.B., Hamre-Nietupski, S., Johnson, F., Wilcox, B., & Gruenwald, L. (1979). A rationale for comprehensive longitudinal interactions between severely handicapped students and nonhandicapped students and other citizens. *AAESPH Review, 4,* 3-14.

Brown, L.F., Branston-McLean, M.B., Baumgart, D., Vincent, L., Falvey, M., & Schroder, J. (1979). Using the characteristics of current and subsequent least restrictive environments in the development of curricular content for severely handicapped students. *Journal of the Association for the Severely Handicapped, 4,* 407-424.

Brown, L.F., Nietupski, J., & Hamre-Nietupski, S. (1976). The criterion of ultimate functioning and public school services for severely handicapped students. In M.A. Thomas (Ed.), *Hey don't forget about me. Education's investment in the severely, profoundly, and multiply handicapped* (pp. 2-15). Reston, VA: Council for Exceptional Children.

Bruner, J.S. (1962). *On knowing: Essays for the left hand.* Cambridge, MA: The Belknap Press of Harvard University Press.

Burns, P.C., Roe, B.D., & Ross, E.P. (1984). *Teaching reading in today's elementary schools.* Boston: Houghton Mifflin.

Cain, S.E., & Evans, J.M. (1984). *Sciencing: An involvement approach to elementary science methods* (2nd ed.). Columbus, OH: Merrill.

Christenson, S.L., & Ysseldyke, J.E. (1989). Assessing student performance: An important change is needed. *Journal of School Psychology, 27,* 409-426.

Clark, G.M. (1979). *Career education for the handicapped child in the elementary classroom.* Denver: Love Publishing.

Collahan, C.M., & Corvo, M.L. (1980). Validating the Ross Test for identification and evaluation of critical thinking skills in programs for the gifted. *Journal of the Education of the Gifted, 4,* 17-22.

Collier, C. (1988). *Assessing minority students with learning and behavior problems.* Lindale, TX: Hamilton Publications.

Cooper, J.D. (1986). *Improving reading comprehension.* Boston: Houghton Mifflin.

Cooper, C.R., & Cooper, R.G. (1984). Skill in peer learning discourse: What develops? In S.A. Kuczaj II (Ed.), *Discourse development* (pp. 77-98). New York: Springer.

Covington, M.V. (1967). Some experimental evidence on teaching creative understanding. *The Reading Teacher, 20,* 390-396.

Craig, H.K. (1983). Applications of pragmatic language models for intervention. In T.M. Gallagher & C.A. Prutting (Eds.), *Pragmatic assessment and intervention issues in language* (pp. 101-127). San Diego: College-Hill Press.

Cronin, M.E., & Gerber, P.J. (1982). Preparing the learning disabled adolescent for adulthood. *Topics in Learning and Learning Disabilities, 2,* 55-68.

D'Angelo, E. (1971). *The teaching of critical thinking*. Amsterdam: B.R. Gruner.

Deno, S.L., & Fuchs, L.S. (1987). Developing curriculum-based measurement systems for data-based special education problem solving. *Focus on Exceptional Children, 19*, 1-16.

Dewey, J. (1910). *Experience and education*. New York: Collier.

Downing, J.A., Ollila, L., & Oliver, P. (1975). Cultural differences in children's concepts of reading and writing. *British Journal of Educational Psychology, 45*, 312-316.

Drew, C.J., Logan, D.R., & Hardman, M.L. (1992). *Mental retardation: A life cycle approach*. New York: Merrill.

Dunn, R. (1984). Learning style: State of the science. *Theory and Practice, 23*, 10-19.

Durkin, D. (1981). What is the value of new interest in reading comprehension? *Language Arts, 58*, 23-43.

Eisenson, J., & Ogilvie, M. (1983). *Communicative disorders in children*. New York: Macmillan.

Eiserman, W.D. (1988). Three types of peer tutoring: Effects on the attitudes of students with learning disabilities and their regular class peers. *Journal of Learning Disabilities, 24*, 223-229.

Ellis, D.B. (1985). *Becoming a master student* (5th ed.). Rapid City, SD: College Survival Inc.

Ennis, R.H. (1962). A concept of critical thinking. *Harvard Educational Review, 32*, 81-88.

Fain, G.S. (1986). Leisure: A moral imperative. *Mental Retardation, 24*, 261-283.

Flavell, J.H. (1963). *The developmental psychology of Jean Piaget*. Princeton, NJ: Van Nostrand.

Franklin, B. (1961). Benjamin Franklin's memoirs. In L.J. Lemisch. *Benjamin Franklin: The autobiography and other writings* (pp. 28-29). New York: Signet Classic.

Gearheart, C., & Gearheart, B. (1990). *Introduction to special education: Principles and practices*. Denver: Love Publishing.

Gickling, E.,& Thompson, V. (1985). A personal view of curriculum-based assessment. *Exceptional Children, 52*, 205-218.

Grossman, H.J. (1983). *Classification in mental retardation*. Washington, DC: American Association on Mental Deficiency.

Guerin, G.R., & Maier, A.S. (1983) *Informal assessment in education*. Palo Alto, CA: Mayfield Publishing.

Guildford, J.P. (1967). Creativity and learning. In D.B. Lindsley & A.A. Lunsdaine (Eds.), *Brain functions: Vol IV. Brain functions and learning* (pp. 34-55). Berkeley, CA: University of California Press.

Hargrove, L.J., & Poteet, J.A. (1984). *Assessment in special education: The education evaluation*. Englewood Cliffs, NJ: Prentice-Hall.

Harris, L.A., & Smith, C.B. (1980). *Reading instruction: Diagnostic teaching in the classroom* (3rd ed.). New York: Holt, Rinehart & Winston.

Hasazi, S.B., Johnson, R.E., Gordon, L.R., & Hull, M. (1989).A statewide follow-up survey of high school exiters: A comparison of former students with and without handicaps. *Journal of Special Education, 20*, 243-255.

Heal, L.W., Sigelman, C.K., & Switzky, H.N. (1978). Research on community residential alternatives for the mentally retarded. *International Review of Research on Mental Retardation, 9*, 209-249.

Heller, M. (1986). How do you know what you know? Metacognition in the content areas. *Journal of Reading Research, 29*, 415-422.

Holdaway, D. (1979). *The foundations of literacy.* New York: Ashton Scholastic.

Howell, K.W., & Morehead, M.K. (1987). *Curriculum-based evaluation for special and remedial education.* Columbus, OH: Merrill.

Huey, E.B. (1968). *The psychology and pedagogy of reading.* Cambridge, MA: MIT Press.

Hunt, J. McV. (1961). *Intelligence and experience.* New York: The Ronald Press.

Jagger, A.M., & Smith-Burke, T. (1985). *Observing the language learner.* Urbana, IL: National Council of the Teachers of English.

Johnson, D.W., Johnson, R.T., & Maruyama, G. (1983). Interdependence and interpersonal attraction among heterogeneous and homogeneous individuals: A theoretical formulation and meta-analysis of the research. *Review of Educational Research, 53*, 5-54.

Jolly, T. (1980). Listen my children and you shall read. *Language Arts, 57*, 214-217.

Jones, L.L. (1982). An interactive view of reading: Implications for the classroom. *The Reading Teacher, 35*, 772-777.

Kavale, K.A. (1980). Reasoning abilities of normal and learning disabled readers on measures of reading comprehension. *Learning Disability Quarterly. 3*, 34-35.

Kirk, S.A., & Gallagher, J.J. (1989). *Educating exceptional children* (6th ed.). Boston: Houghton Mifflin.

Kokaska, C.J., & Brolin, D.E. (1985). *Career education for handicapped individuals* (2nd ed.). Columbus, OH: Merrill.

Lamberg, W.J., & Lamb, C.E. (1980). *Reading instruction in the content areas.* Boston: Houghton Mifflin.

Lamkin, J.S. (1980). *Getting started: Career education activities for exceptional students. (K-9).* Reston, VA: The Council for Exceptional Children.

Landerholm, E. (1990). The transdisciplinary team approach in infant intervention programs. *Teaching Exceptional Children, 22*, 66-70.

Lerner, J. (1989). *Learning disabilities: Theories, diagnosis, and teaching strategies* (5th ed.). Boston: Houghton Mifflin.

Lloyd, J., Crowley, E., Kohler, F., & Strain, P. (1988). Redefining the applied research agenda: Cooperative learning, prereferral teacher consultation, and peer-mediated interventions. *Journal of Learning Disabilities, 21*, 43-52.

Loban, W.D. (1963). *The language of elementary school children.* Champaign, IL: National Council of Teachers of English.

Loban, W.D. (1976). *Language development: Kindergarten through grade twelve.* Urbana, IL: National Council of Teachers of English.

Lundsteen, S.W. (1989). *Language arts: A problem solving approach.* New York: Harper & Row.

McCullough, C.M. (1957). Responses of elementary school children to common types of reading comprehension questions. *Journal of Educational Research, 51*, 65-70.

McLeod, T., & Armstrong, S. (1982). Learning disabilities in mathematics: Skill deficits and remedial approaches at the intermediate and secondary level. *Learning Disability Quarterly, 5*, 305-311.

References 209

McLoughlin, J.A., & Lewis, R.B. (1990). *Assessing special students* (3rd ed.). Columbus, OH: Charles E. Merrill.

McNeil, J.D. (1992). *Reading comprehension: New directions for classroom practice* (3rd ed). Los Angeles: HarperCollins.

McPeck, J.E. (1981). *Critical thinking and education.* New York: St. Martin's Press.

Menyuk, P. (1984). Language development and reading. In J. Flood (Ed.), *Understanding comprehension* (pp. 101-121). Newark, DE: International Reading Association.

Mercer, C.D. (1991). *Students with learning disabilities* (4th ed.). New York: Merrill.

Mithaug, D.E., Horiuchi, C.N., & Fanning, P.N. (1985). A report on the Colorado statewide follow-up survey of special education students. *Exceptional Children, 51,* 397-404.

Montague, E.J., Huntsberger, J., & Hoffman, J. (1989). *Fundamentals of elementary and middle school classroom instruction.* Columbus, OH: Merrill.

Myers, M. (1983). Approaches to the teaching of composition. In M. Myers & J. Gray, *Theory and practice in teaching composition: Processing, distancing and modeling* (pp. 3-43). Urbana, IL: National Council of Teachers of English.

Napell, S.M. (1978). Using questions to enhance classroom learning. *Education, 99,* 188-197.

National Assessment of Educational Progress. (1976). *Reading and literature general information yearbook.* Washington, DC: United States Government Printing Office.

National Council of Supervisors of Mathematics. (1977). Position paper on basic mathematical skills. *The Arithmetic Teacher, 25,* 19-22.

Norton, D.E. (1989). *The effective teaching of the language arts* (3rd ed.). Columbus, OH: Merrill.

Olson, J., & Platt, J. (1992). *Teaching children and adolescents with special needs.* New York: Merrill.

Overton, T. (1992). *Assessment in special education: An applied approach.* New York: Merrill.

Palincsar, A., & Brown, A. (1984). *Reciprocal teaching of comprehension monitoring activities* (Technical Rep. No. 269). Champaign, IL: University of Illinois Center for the Study of Reading.

Paris, S., & Myers, M. (1981). Comprehension monitoring, memory and study strategies of good and poor readers. *Journal of Reading Behavior, 13,* 5-22.

Paris, S.G., Wasik, B.A., & Turner, J.C. (1991). The development of strategic readers. In R. Burr, M. Kaamil, P. Rosenthal, & P.D. Pearson (Eds.), *The handbook of reading research. Vol. 11* (pp. 606-620). New York: Longman.

Patton, J.R., Beirne-Smith, M., & Payne, J.S. (1990). *Mental retardation* (3rd ed.). Columbus, OH: Merrill.

Pearson, P.D. (1979). *The effect of background knowledge on young children's comprehension of explicit and implicit information.* Urbana, IL: University of Illinois Center for the Study of Reading.

Pearson, P.D., & Johnson, D.D. (1977). *Teaching reading comprehension.* New York: Holt, Rinehart & Winston.

Piaget, J. (1963). *The origins of intelligence in children.* New York: Norton.

Piaget, J. (1964). The Piaget papers. In R.E. Ripple & J.N. Rockcastel (Eds.), *Piaget rediscovered.* A report of the Conference on Cognitive Studies and Curriculum Development. Ithaca, NY: School of Education, Cornell University.

Piaget, J. (1969). *The theory of stages in cognitive development.* Monterey, CA: CTB/McGraw-Hill.

Piaget, J. (1975). *The development of thought: Equilibration of cognitive structures.* New York: Viking Press.

Polloway, E.A., Patton, J.R., Payne, J.S., & Payne, R.A. (1989). *Strategies for teaching learners with special needs* (4th ed.). New York: Merrill.

Polloway, E.A., & Smith, T.E.C. (1992). *Language instruction for students with disabilities* (2nd ed.). Denver: Love Publishing.

Posner, M.J. (1982). *Executive essentials.* New York: Avon.

Reid, D.K. (1988). *Teaching the learning disabled: A cognitive development approach.* Boston: Allyn & Bacon.

Robinson, H.M. (1964). Developing critical readers. In R.G. Stauffer, *Dimensions of critical reading.* XI. (pp. 1-11). Newark, DE: University of Delaware Proceedings of the Annual Education and Reading Conferences.

Roe, B.D., Stoodt, B.S., & Burns, P.C. (1991). *Secondary school reading instruction: The content areas* (4th ed.). Boston: Houghton Mifflin.

Romanish, B. (1986). Critical thinking and the curriculum: A critique. *The Educational Forum, 51,* 45-56.

Roser, N.L. (1984). Teaching and testing reading comprehension: An historical perspective on instructional research and practices. In J. Flood (Ed.), *Promoting reading comprehension* (pp. 48-60). Newark, DE: International Reading Association.

Rubin, D. (1992). *Teaching reading and study skills in content areas.* Boston: Allyn & Bacon.

Russell, D.H. (1956). *Children's thinking.* Boston: Ginn.

Salvia, J., & Ysseldyke, J.E. (1988). *Assessment in special and remedial education* (4th ed.) Boston: Houghton Mifflin.

Schuler, L., Ogulthorpe, R.T., & Eiserman, W.D. (1987). The effects of reverse-role tutoring on the social acceptance of students with behavioral disorders. *Behavioral Disorders, 13,* 35-44.

Schuster, J.W., & Griffen, A.K. (1990). Using time delay with task analyses. *Teaching Exceptional Children, 22,* 49-53.

Scruggs, T.E., Mastropieri, M.A., Veit, D.T., & Ogulthorpe, R.T. (1986). Behaviorally disordered students as tutors: Effects on social behaviors. *Behavioral Disorders, 12,* 36-44.

Scruggs, T.E., & Richter, L. (1986). Tutoring learning disabled students: A critical review. *Learning Disabilities Quarterly, 9,* 2-14.

Siegler, R.S. (1983). Information processing approaches to cognitive development. In W. Kesson (Ed.), *Handbook of child psychology: History, theory, and methods. Vol. 1* (pp. 129-211). New York: Wiley.

Sigel, I., & Hooper, F. (Eds.). (1968). *Logical thinking in children.* New York: Holt, Rinehart and Winston.

Slavin, R.E. (1988). *Student team learning: An overview and practical guide* (2nd ed.). Washington, DC: National Education Association.

Slavin, R.E., Leavey, M., & Madden, N.A. (1984). Combining cooperative learning and individualized instruction: Effects on student mathematics achievement, attitudes, and behaviors. *Elementary School Journal, 84,* 409-422.

Smith, B.E., Goodman, K.S., & Meredith, R. (1976). *Language and thinking in the schools* (2nd ed.). New York: Holt, Rinehart and Winston.

Smith, F. (1975). *Comprehension and learning: A conceptual framework for teachers.* New York: Holt, Rinehart and Winston.

Smoot, S.L. (1985). Exercise programs for mainstreamed handicapped students. *Teaching Exceptional Children, 17,* 262-266.

Stauffer, R.G. (1969). *Directing reading maturity: As a cognitive process.* New York: Harper and Row.

Stiggins, R.J. (1985). Improving assessment where it means the most: In the classroom. *Educational Leadership, 43,* 69-74.

Swanson, H.L., & Watson, B.L. (1982). *Educational and psychological assessment of exceptional children: Theories, strategies, and applications.* St. Louis, MO: C.V. Mosby.

Thomas, A., & Chess, S. (1977). *Temperament and development.* New York: Brunner/Mazel.

Tompkins, G.E., & Hoskisson, K. (1991). *Language arts: Content and teaching strategies.* New York: Macmillan.

Tonjes, M.J., & Zintz, M.V. (1981). *Teaching reading/thinking/study skills in content classrooms.* Dubuque, IA: William C. Brown.

Torgesen, J.K. (1979). Factors related to poor performance on memory tasks in reading disabled children. *Learning Disability Quarterly, 2,* 17-23.

Valletutti, P.J., & Bender, M. (1982). *Teaching interpersonal and community living skills: A curriculum model for handicapped adolescents and adults.* Baltimore: University Park Press.

Valletutti, P.J., & Bender, M. (1985). *Teaching the moderately and severely handicapped: Curriculum objectives, strategies, and activities. Vol 2. Communication and socialization.* Austin, TX: PRO-ED.

Valletutti, P., & Christoplos, F. (1990). Giochi cooperativi per l'integrazione degli alunni handicappati. [Cooperative academic games for integrating handicapped students]. *Insegnare all' Handicappato, 4,* 153-162.

Valletutti, P.J., & Salpino, A.O. (1979). *Individualizing educational objectives and programs: A modular approach.* Baltimore: University Park Press.

Vygotsky, L.S. (1934). *Thought and language.* Cambridge, MA: The MIT Press.

Vygotsky, L.S. (1962). *Thought and language.* New York: Wiley.

Wallas, G. (1926). *The art of thought.* New York: Harcourt Brace.

Wehman, P., & Kregel, J. (1985). A supported work approach to competitive employment of individuals with moderate and severe handicaps. *Journal of the Association for Persons with Severe Handicaps, 10,* 3-11.

Wehman, P., Kregel, J., & Barcus, J.M. (1985). Transition from school to work for individuals with severe disabilities: A follow-up study. In P. Wehman & J. W. Hill (Eds.), *Competitive employment for persons with mental retardation: From research to practice* (pp. 247-264). Richmond: Rehabilitation Research and Training Center, Virginia Commonwealth University.

Willbrand, M.L., & Rieke, R.D. (1983). *Teaching oral communication.* New York: Macmillan.

Wixson, K.K, Bosky, A.B., Yochum, M.N., & Alvermann, D.E. (1984). An interview for assessing students' perceptions of classroom reading tasks. *Reading Teacher, 37*, 346-353.

Wolf, W., Huck, C., & King, M. (1967). *The critical reading ability of elementary school children*. Columbus, OH: Ohio State University Research Foundation. Project No. 5-1040

Woodruff, A.D. (1961). *Basic concepts of teaching*. San Francisco: Chandler.

Young, W.E. (1936). The relation of reading comprehension and retention to hearing comprehension and retention. *Journal of Exceptional Education, 5*, 30-39.

Ysseldyke, J.E., Algozzine, B., & Thurlow, M.L. (1992). *Critical issues in special education* (2nd ed.). Boston: Houghton Mifflin.

Zintz, M.V. (1970). *The reading process: The teacher and the learner*. Dubuque, IA: William C. Brown.

INDEX